"THE GREATEST LIFE EVER LIVED . . .

. . . was the life of Jesus. The greatest teachings ever given to man came from the lips of Jesus Christ. Today he stands again at the point where all the roads of humanity meet."

The simple and effective information contained in this book is offered by the author in the hope that those who come to know more about Jesus will also come to know him better as Lord and Master of all life.

LIFE AND TEACHINGS OF JESUS

T. Franklin Miller

THE WARNER PRESS   Anderson, Indiana

*This book is dedicated to my mother, and to the
memory of my father, who first taught me by careful
precept and noble example the meaning of a life
centered in Jesus Christ.*

The New Testament passages in this book are quoted from the
Revised Standard Version of the New Testament, copyrighted in
1946 by the Division of Christian Education of NCCCUSA and are
used by permission.

LIFE AND TEACHINGS OF JESUS

A WARNER PRESS BOOK
Published for Warner Press, Inc., by Pyramid Publications

This edition published April, 1971

Reprinted September, 1983

Library of Congress Catalog Card Number: 59-13465

ISBN   0-87162-114-2

Printed in the United States of America

WARNER PRESS BOOKS are published by Warner Press, Inc.
1200 East 5th Street, Anderson, Indiana 46011, U.S.A.

CONTENTS

PREFACE

The greatest life ever lived was the life of Jesus. The greatest teachings ever given to man came from the lips of Jesus Christ. For nineteen hundred years He has haunted the literature of the world. Today he stands again at the point where all the roads of humanity meet, waiting to be made Lord and King of all who will accept him.

Teaching the life of Jesus to boys and girls and to youth and adults may become one of the most effective ministries any person could ever desire. It is to help those who teach that this book has been written. It has been prepared with the hope that it may be of some service in the field of general reading, but more especially in the field of church-school teaching.

This book makes no claim whatever of dealing with the problems which are presented in a critical study of the life of Jesus. It aims at giving a brief overview of that life and of the teachings of Jesus, more to introduce the teacher to the interesting and rewarding experience which a critical and detailed study would bring than to close the door to such an experience.

The author feels a strong indebtedness to many friends for invaluable suggestions and wise counsel, to those who have written other books dealing with the life of Jesus, and to a great host of church school workers whose comments and suggestions not only encouraged the writing of this book but were most helpful in determining the format and the approach of this study of Jesus and his teachings.

This book is offered with the knowledge that no book about Jesus or his teachings can ever substitute for a personal commitment to Jesus Christ. It is the writer's hope that those who come to know more about him will also come to know him better as Lord and Master of all life.

T. FRANKLIN MILLER

Chapter I

THE WORLD
INTO WHICH JESUS CAME

A group of English literary leaders were discussing persons they would like to have met—persons who had walked across the pages of history and now were dead but not forgotten. One writer wanted to see Julius Caesar, another Judas Iscariot, while a third wanted to meet Moses. As they talked on, still another person said he would like to have seen King Solomon, and another wished he could have met Alexander the Great. Finally, Samuel Johnson said, "If any of these persons were to enter the room, we should all stand and greet him with proud acclaim; but I should like to have seen a man who, if he entered this room would cause me to bow and kiss the hem of his garment."

We know that Johnson referred to Jesus of Nazareth. And do not all of us feel that way about him?

In a world trembling with fear of its own power gone berserk, this strange Man of Galilee is our ultimate hope of peace and of salvation. He still walks among us to press home to all men of all nations his claim to their supreme allegiance, and as they yield to the power of his redemptive love men still are changed into the likeness of the Son of God.

We shall never cease writing and talking about Jesus, nor shall we cease singing about him and worshiping him. He is the central and most important figure in the one movement that is more elevating to mankind than all other movements combined. He is the supreme figure of all history.

Jesus is also the enigma of history. His life has never been adequately described, although the writers of the New Testament Gospels and a host of writers since have exhausted their vocabularies in trying. We cannot fully understand him; we can only hope that through prayerful and careful study we shall be able to understand him better.

The life of Jesus cannot be understood in isolation, but only in relation to the whole society of nineteen centuries ago. It is most important that one should know something of the people who were Jesus' associates and contemporaries and the general conditions under which they lived. So this study of the life of Jesus will begin with a brief survey of the political, economic, social and religious background.

THE POLITICAL BACKGROUND

The location of Palestine had much to do with the fortunes and misfortunes of the Jews for many centuries. The Promised Land to which Moses led his people from Egypt was the crossroads of important trade routes; certain parts of it had fertile soil, and many things could be said in its favor. But this narrow strip of land lay as a buffer state between powerful and aggressive nations. When the land of the Israelites lay in the path of expansion, the big powers used it as a political football. Centuries of living under the threat of war or under oppression left their certain mark upon the religious and social life of the Jews.

Before 933 B.C. the Hebrew state was a united monarchy, but in that year the United Kingdom became divided and the Hebrew state as such began its long, slow decline in a gradual but certain political deterioration. The Northern Kingdom was plundered first, and in the torturous years that followed Judah also fell. In slow succession the Jews were dominated by the Assyrians, Babylonians, Persians, Greeks, and Romans. The Jewish state really ceased to exist as such when Pompey took Palestine and made it subject to Rome in 63 B.C.

The Maccabees

One intense thrust for freedom came during the second century before Christ under the three Maccabees, John Hyrcanus, Judas Aristobulus, and Alexander Jannaeus. The Maccabees took the tiny and insignificant district of Judea and enlarged its boundaries until it was almost as large as the kingdom under David. The Maccabees used forced conversions to Judaize the conquered peoples, for it would seem that unless the Jews had become a power strong enough for the Romans to take them seriously they always would have remained insignificant in the family of nations.

At any rate, whatever the Maccabees were able to gain was all lost after the conquest by Romans and when Herod the Great came to the throne of Judea.

Rule of Herod the Great

Herod the Great ruled from 37 to 4 B.C. He ascended to the throne only after thirty years of war that climaxed in a long siege of Jerusalem and bloody contests between Herod and Mattathias Antigonus, the last king of pure Maccabean stock. One historian states that in the thirty years of bloodshed from 67 to 37 B.C. Jerusalem and the entire land of Israel was reduced to a wilderness, and more than a hundred thousand Jews were killed. Those who remained were gripped by either a feeble and passive despair that saw no possible hope, or the "bitter-minded despair" of religious fanaticism that was willing to risk anything to bring a change for the better.

Herod sought to bring the Greek influence into Judea, yet whenever it was possible he did try to please the Jews. He kept an ear to the ground, but more often than not he used force instead of diplomacy to enforce his rule. He was a builder, and apparently sought to restore the country that had been so wantonly devastated. He constructed roads and aqueducts, palaces and theaters, and in 20 B.C. he began to rebuild the Jewish Temple at Jerusalem.

Herod the Great was unspeakably cruel. He inflicted heavy taxes to pay for his public works program. One historian says of him: "He stole along to his throne like a fox; he ruled like a tiger, and died like a dog." He did not promote much warfare with other countries, yet his oppression brought intense suffering to the Jews. He lived in debauchery and contempt for law, openly flattering the wealthy who courted his favor and murdering those who crossed him. Coming as he did so close to the birth of Jesus, he only intensified the Jewish longing for a deliverer and a Messiah.

The Roman Tetrarchies

After the death of Herod the Great the country was divided into three districts, called tetrarchies, each governed by a tetrarch who, during the time of Jesus, was replaced by a procurator.

Herod Philip received Trachonitus and Iturea. There was a fairly high state of ciivlization in the Decapolis, which showed dominant Greek influence. Philip was peaceful and the most respectable of the three sons of Herod the Great. Three years after the death of Philip, or in A.D. 37, this Roman province came under the control of Herod Agrippa, who also figured in New Testament history.

Galilee and Perea were given to Herod Antipas, whom Jesus called "that fox." The inhabitants of Perea were a mixture of Jews and Gentiles, while Galilee had been Jewish for about one hundred years. In the latter province was Nazareth, the boyhood home of Jesus, located just a few miles distant from the Roman capital, Sepphoris. Galilee was dotted with literally hundreds of small villages, all of which had bloodshed, war, revolt, and murder as household words. If the people had not suffered these distresses at the hands of their oppressors, they would have suffered the same from attacks by the bands of brigands or zealots who lived in caves, led fierce but ineffective revolts, and pillaged and ravaged those who opposed their fight for freedom. Herod Antipas had some knowledge about Jesus and John the Baptist, and one of his officials had a wife who was a follower of Jesus.

The most important political divisions of the land, Samaria and Judea, went to Archelaus. Between the Jews and the Samaritans there was never anything but bitterness, suspicion, hostility, and hatred. Archelaus was guilty of atrocities toward both Jews and Samaritans, and after ten years was called to Rome by the enraged emperor, who removed him from office. Judea, Samaria, and Idumea were later attached to Syria, with a Roman procurator or commissioner in charge.

Supposedly, the high priest was the leader of the Jewish people, but under Herod the Great the high priests had lost whatever power they had enjoyed, and he appointed and deposed them at will. After Archelaus was removed from office, the Romans appointed a procurator who was subject to the governor of Syria, but who was responsible for administering the affairs of the Jews. Much of the work was left to the high priest, but the procurator had to be consulted before any important step could be taken. He lived in Caesarea and went to Jerusalem for the important days of religious festivals or similar occasions. He maintained a permanent Roman army in Jerusalem.

Some of the procurators, such as Pontius Pilate, seized every occasion to show contempt and disdain for the Jews, while other officials sometimes took the attitude that all would be well if the Jews paid their taxes and kept quiet. Customs in the border towns were collected by publicans; these receipts and other taxes collected by tax gatherers were sent to the procurator as the chief financial agent of the state. Life under Roman rule was galling to the Jews. Never did they seek to adjust to

servitude and oppression. They always kept the
freedom of their spirit even though they did live in
a land occupied by military forces.

With such a record of war and chaos through the
preceding centuries, with such turmoil, unrest, bitterness and intense hatred prevalent, with nerves
on edge and with danger and fear on all sides,
Jews everywhere could hope that "the fullness of
time" was near at hand and with it the coming of
the Messiah. Into such a world came Jesus. Into a
world of war and hatred, tumult and trouble, came
Jesus, the Prince of Peace. He came preaching that
men were born to be the sons of God. He came
with hope for the hopeless and light for the blind.

The Economic Background

The Caesars had welded their farflung domin-
ions into one political empire, but it was an expensive operation. To the staggering costs of wars
must be added the cost of maintaining standing ar-
mies in strategic spots. In Palestine prosperity had
faded into gaunt, terrible poverty. Taxes, both civil
and religious, were unbearable, but necessary to
support the overhead machinery of corrupt ecclesi-
asticism and of extravagant courts of luxury.

There were wealthy people, else we would not
have had the story of the rich man and Lazarus or
the rich young ruler. In almost every case wealth
represented some exploitation of the poor laborers.
Many of the Sadducees were in this class. The high
priests and their family connections were in control
of the wealth. There probably were not many land-
ed estates in Palestine, but some did exist. The
Gospels give us the parable of the owner who went
to a far country and entrusted his estate to the care

of his stewards. It is not likely, though, that there were many men of great wealth during the days of Jesus, which followed the Herodian exploitation of all the resources of the land of Israel.

The Poor

There probably was a well-to-do class of peasants, and there were the poor. There were those who had no means of income except as they were able to hire themselves out a day at a time. Besides these day laborers there were some craftsmen who employed apprentices. There were some tenant farmers, and there must have been at least occasional strife between the tenant and the owner, as one would surmise from the account Matthew gives of the wicked husbandman. There was also a class of peasants who owned just enough land to meet family needs by doing all the work themselves.

Of the poor people there must have been many. Those who could not support themselves on small tracts of land or by a trade became "hirelings," and those who could not find work were reduced to begging. Many of the blind and crippled became beggars because there was nothing else for them to do. Jesus had patience and sympathy for the beggars. Where could sharper contrast be drawn than in the picture Jesus gives of "a certain rich man" living in luxury, and a beggar named Lazarus who sat at his gate, "full of sores"?

Many of the parables of Jesus and many of the incidents of his life take on new meaning if one can read them with some knowledge of how people made their living, what crops they grew, how commerce and trade were carried on, and what social cleavages created tension.

Slaves and Slavery

There were two classes of slaves. It is difficult for a twentieth-century reader to picture the lot of the slave in the day of Jesus, or to imagine the social impact of Jesus' vowed intention to "set at liberty them that are bound." The Canaanitish slaves, who came from Tyre and Sidon, were the most despised. There were not so many Hebrew slaves in Palestine, but they must have helped to intensify the upheavals that crowded the tumultuous days of the early Christian Era. Slaves belonged to their masters as chattel property. A slave had no rights of his own. The one thing that marked a slave as different from an animal was that under certain rules a master who beat his slave to death might himself be put to death.

The taxes were always present. Export and import taxes were collected by the publicans or tax collectors. These men had fallen into such disrepute that from the time of Herod the term "publican" meant robber, murderer, or thief. This frontier tax became an obstacle to commerce. Every city or province had its border tax, which inflated the cost of merchandise beyond all reason. Even so, many Jews at the time of Jesus were engaged in commerce and trade, and every city and town had its booths where all sorts of wares were offered for sale. Rome collected taxes at every turn of the road; there was a water tax, a city tax, a road tax, a salt tax, a house tax, a meat tax, and so on and on. Against all of these taxes the Jews rebelled at heart; some led local, open rebellion, while others waited in their silent suffering for the coming of the Messiah.

A word should be said about the Roman troops stationed in Palestine. These were troops from other provinces, and their leaders did not understand the Jews. There was friction, and the Jews were under constant humiliation that these symbols of oppression remained to taunt and harass them.

RELIGIOUS LIFE AMONG THE JEWS

God and Angels

All Jews believed in a God who was holy and righteous, eternal, living, and all-powerful. God was so holy that his name should not be spoken by any person. He was the God of Abraham and of Isaac and of Jacob; he was their own God, too, and any humble Jew could turn to him in prayer for help and consolation. The Jews were familiar with the phrase Jesus used in the prayer, "Our Father who art in heaven," which perhaps is one reason why Jesus chose it.

The Jews also believed that God was surrounded by angels, who served as messengers for him and to enhance the beauty of the heavenly court. An innumerable company of these spirits, or angels, had been created on the second day of creation, and God created more angels as they were needed.

There were angels in heaven, and there were fallen angels who had refused to do the will of God. Beelzebub was the ruler or leader of the fallen angels and was head of the kingdom that stood in opposition to the kingdom of God.

Sin, Repentance, and Forgiveness

The Jews knew there is a constant struggle within man—right and wrong fighting for supremacy and control of the personality. They knew that their God was a God of wrath and of stern judgment, but that repentance would bring forgiveness. John the Baptist and Jesus both stressed repentance in their messages, and Jesus went beyond to show the tender and forgiving love of the Father.

The Law

There really were two "laws." There was the written law, or the Law of Moses, which appears in our Bibles as the first five books of the Old Testament, or the Pentateuch. This was called the Torah by the Jews, and they believed that having it in their possession indicated that God had chosen them for a special purpose. Keeping the Law, then, was a delight and not a burden to a devout and reverent Jew.

In addition to the written law, there was the oral law, or the traditions of the elders, later gathered into one book and called the Mishnah. The Pharisees placed both laws on an equal basis, but the Sadducees did not give the same authority to the oral law as they allowed for the Law of Moses. The oral law had two parts: the precepts, which were defined by the rabbis, and the explanations or further interpretations. Some of the teachings of Jesus and the conflicts he had with Sadducees and Pharisees can be understood only when we know something of the ramifications of law and authority among the Jews.

Religion to the Jews was a *way* of life, a matter

of right conduct. In contrast to this Jesus said he came to bring *life*, and that *he* was the way of life. To conform to the Law, the Jew was circumcised, he kept the Sabbath, and he observed ceremonial laws regarding the preparation and eating of food. A devout Jew did not eat with non-Jews nor with those who were ceremonially unclean. Food must be not only sanitary, but ceremonially clean. To observe the Sabbath, the Jew had to know what was work and what absolutely necessary work could be performed without breaking the Law. Thus the many, many interpretations and traditions came into being.

No matter what the Christian today may think of these religious observances, to the devout Jew there was nothing in life more important. He felt that life was meaningless unless he could please God, and the way to please God was to keep the Law. For those who held to the traditions, then, keeping the Law involved every act of life and every minute of every day.

The Temple and Teaching

The institutional center of the Jewish religion was the Temple in Jerusalem. It was here that the three major feasts were celebrated, although devout Jews who could not come to Jerusalem had appropriate observances in their homes and synagogues. The Feast of Tabernacles was the harvest festival, held in the fall of the year. In the spring there was the Feast of the Passover and its accompanying Feast of Unleavened Bread, followed fifty days later by the Feast of Pentecost. To care for the administration of the Temple worship there were thousands of priests, divided into twenty-four orders, each of which worked for one week at a time. During its week of work, the order distributed individual responsibility by the drawing of lots; it was thus that Zechariah was ministering in the Temple when the announcement came that he should have a son.

To support the huge retinue of Temple workers the Jews brought in their sacrifices, tithes, offerings, vows, and Temple tax, which in fact made the Temple a sort of Bank of Jerusalem. Since the priests controlled the wealth, they literally controlled society in Jerusalem. During the three feasts enormous crowds of pilgrims came into Jerusalem from all over the world; to insure that they would have animals without blemish and fit for sacrifice, the priesthood offered animals and doves for sale to the pilgrims, and the bank set up its tables for changing Roman money, which bore the image of Caesar, into the coin of the Temple. Since the incoming Jews had no choice, exorbitant rates were often charged for changing money and for the animals for sacrifice; it was against this highhanded robbery and unfair exploitation of a religious motive and ceremony that Jesus spoke in his denunciation at the cleansing of the Temple.

The Synagogue

Wherever as many as ten Jews could come together, a synagogue could be established. It was a center of worship and of teaching in the local community. Services were often held in the evening, and of course on the Sabbath. The rabbi taught the boys of the village during the day. It was the custom of Jesus to visit the synagogue regularly, and on some occasions he read from the Law and interpreted the passage to his hearers. The synagogue was really the center of religious nurture and spiritual culture for the common people.

THE RELIGIOUS PARTIES IN PALESTINE

The Pharisees

The Pharisees were the popular religious party of the day in which Jesus lived. Just as in any religious group, so among the Pharisees there were some who were a credit to the group and others who brought reproach upon it. Jesus apparently came into contact often with those who brought no credit to their group. He attacked them severely, condemned them for preaching the good but not practicing it, and charged them with being hypocrites.

Jesus charged them with neglect of the weighty matters of the Law while they gave careful attention to the detailed observance of it. They were the ones who had developed the tradition of the fathers, which gave to the people of Israel hundreds of rules for ceremonial observances not found in the Law of Moses. It was in obeying these detailed laws that the Pharisees missed the more important part of the Law of Moses, which had to do with an inner motivation for righteousness. They gave the impression to the common people that careful observance of the ceremonial laws was more important than ethical living. Indeed, according to the interpretation given by the Pharisees, the common man of the street simply could not be religious; often he could not read, hence he could not know the vast number of religious ordinances he was supposed to obey in the ceremonial law.

The Sadducees

The well-born families, for the most part, and those who had priestly connections belonged to the Sadducees. They were the wealthy and official party of Jews, and had come to be known for their sympathy to the Hellenist, or Greek, influences. They were just as careful as were the Pharisees to insist upon an exact observance of trivial ceremonial details. The difference, however, came at the point of the law which they recognized. For the Pharisees it was the tradition of the fathers, sometimes called the oral law, while the Sadducees recognized the authority only of the written law.

The Sadducees were severe in judgment and often cruel, even toward each other, whereas the Pharisees lived on somewhat more friendly terms with their own group. The Sadducees taught that there is no resurrection from the dead, but that the soul dies with the body. They believed that man as an individual is responsible for his own actions; if he achieves happiness, he has himself to thank, and if he is unhappy, he alone is responsible for his misery.

It is difficult for us to realize with what profound concern the Sadducees and Pharisees insisted upon the detailed observance of trivial religious duties. To them, though, there was nothing trivial about the multitudinous rules, and we can only with difficulty appreciate how that attitude and belief affected everything they did and all their manner of life. Small wonder that Jesus came into such sharp conflict with these two religious groups!

The Essenes

The Essenes were a small, closely knit religious sect which resembled a secret order established on a communal pattern. They were intensely nationalistic, and probably numbered less than four thousand at the time Jesus lived. They were ascetics, living very simply, with strict regard for certain ceremonial observances; they believed in labor and manual work for all and were opposed to bloodshed even in the offering of sacrifices. The Essenes practiced a socialism that was positive in its approach, with equality of members and common sharing of all property.

Through the years there have been efforts to identify Jesus with various of these religious groups; especially strong attempts have been made to identify him with the Essenes. However, John the Baptist and some of the disciples of Jesus probably were far more influenced by the Essenes than was Jesus, who was not concerned about forming a community of ascetics, but wanted all men to share in the good things of God.

The Zealots

This group was the opposite of the Essenes. The Zealots promoted a socialism that was to be instituted by force and violence. The Zealots had a majority of younger men in their number. They were also intensely nationalistic, inflamed with a great religious and political idea for which they were ready to lay down their lives. Among the Zealots were to be found the outstanding warriors of Israel.

The Zealots were Pharisees who had gone to the

extreme position of adding to their love for the written and oral law their extreme zeal for protecting the law with the sword. They were strong in Galilee, numbering probably tens of thousands of followers. These religious fanatics often grouped into small bands, ready to strike a blow for freedom against their hated Roman rulers.

Among the disciples of Jesus was Simon the Zealot, and it is probable that many other Zealots followed Jesus with the hope that he might be the Messiah who would overthrow the Romans and bring in a kingdom by violence. It probably was to this point that Jesus spoke in Matthew 11:12, "From the days of John the Baptist until now the kingdom of heaven suffereth violence, and the violent take it by force."

THE MESSIANIC HOPE

The lot of the Jews was not a happy one, but they looked to God for help. Through their darkest hours there were always prophets or other religious leaders to remind them that hope was not lost, and that God had something infinitely better for the Jews. The Jews could not reconcile their condition with the promises God had made them, and by the time of Jesus there had developed a strong belief that a Messiah would come to deliver them.

There were many variations of the Messianic hope. Some believed a deliverer would come to overthrow all political enemies and set up a new political kingdom. Others thought that all the blessings the Messiah would bring would be spiritual and would occur in an age to come. All of them believed that their Messiah would bring fabulous blessings for the Jews.

The baffling thing about Jesus was that he refused to fit any of the accepted views of the Messiah. He was the Messiah, but he was not the kind of Messiah many Jews expected. This Messianic hope, however, was very strong in the Jews, and served to ripen the time for the coming of Jesus.

JOHN THE BAPTIST

Of the early life of John the Baptist we know very little. Jesus paid high tribute to John, and we do know that many disciples gathered around him, so he must have been an influential person. He was clothed in camel's hair and a leather girdle, which indicates that he thought himself akin to the prophets. His one message was repentance. He did not call for social and political reforms, but was concerned only that people repent and prepare themselves for the coming of the Messiah.

John disagreed with all the religious groups of his time on the coming of the Messiah. They felt Messiah was coming for all orthodox Jews, whereas John preached that only those who repented and brought forth fruit of repentance would be eligible for the blessings of the Kingdom. He preached stern judgment and a day of wrath for those who did not repent and be baptized.

The consideration of the baptism of Jesus will be reserved until the study of the beginning of the early ministry of Jesus.

TOPICS FOR FURTHER THOUGHT

1. Some of the great religions of the world might be called philosophies, but Christianity is essentially an historical religion. How does Christianity differ in this

respect from some other religions? Why is it so necessary to know the history of the Jews in order to understand Jesus and Christianity?

2. Give some reasons why the Jews have so often suffered intense persecution.

3. What was the difference between the Samaritans and the Jews, and why was there such conflict and tension between them?

4. In a Bible dictionary, look up the following words and read the descriptions given: Zealots, Scribes, Herodians, Essenes.

5. Study the four Gospels to discover the attitude of Jesus toward the Pharisees. Were all Pharisees like those to whom Jesus gave so much attention, or were they the exceptional ones?

6. Read all a Bible dictionary has to say about the Maccabees.

7. Can you say why there were so many very poor people in the day of Jesus?

8. Refer to a map of Palestine and locate the following places, trying to identify each place as you locate it: Judea, Samaria, Idumea, Galilee, Perea.

9. The Jews were seeking freedom, and for them it would have to be religious and political freedom. Do you think that true religious freedom can ever be secured and maintained by the use of force?

10. Of the following topics, which would you say occupied the most prominent place in the life of the peasants of Jesus' day? Which was first in the mind of the leaders of the Jewish religion? Taxation, farming, health, economic security, political freedom, social security, religious freedom, spiritual living?

CHAPTER II

AN OUTLINE OF
THE LIFE OF JESUS

CHILDHOOD AND YOUTH

Birth and Infancy

Matthew and Luke tell us that Jesus was born in Bethlehem. Caesar Augustus had decreed that there should be an enrollment or registration of his subjects, and since Joseph belonged to the family of David he and Mary had gone to Bethlehem, the ancestral home, for the registration. The town was crowded with the throngs who had come for the same purpose, and when Joseph arrived the only lodging he could find was in a stable attached to an inn. When Mary gave birth to her baby she laid him in the manger, and to that humble spot came wise men from distant lands and shepherds from near-by fields to adore and worship Jesus.

The world still wonders at the birth of this baby whose coming has made such a difference. There are many things about his birth on which we do not possess complete knowledge, but we still wonder, we still worship, we are hushed at the sign of God in human flesh.

Joseph fled from Bethlehem to Egypt, and thus the child escaped the terrible massacre of infants instigated by Herod in a fit of jealous rage. Later the family returned to Nazareth, and there Jesus grew up.

A Boy in Nazareth

One story from the Gospels tells us that the family of Joseph was devout and well versed in the Law, a religious family that adhered to the religious customs of the day (Luke 2:41-52). Jesus knew the Scriptures so well that we know he must have been carefully schooled in them when he was a child. We do not know for sure that Nazareth had a synagogue school, but surely Jesus attended if there was one. The attitude the religious leaders took toward him in his public ministry indicates that Jesus was not one of the trained scribes of the day, but a religious layman.

Jesus as a Youth

Joseph was a carpenter by trade, and Jesus followed the same occupation. It is probable that Joseph died while Jesus was yet a young man, and that the support of the family fell largely to Jesus. He was of the common class of people who were accustomed to honest toil; Jesus was a friend of the poor, for he had experienced their poverty, their toil, their trouble.

A reading of the parables and teachings of Jesus gives some insight into the influences which probably surrounded Jesus all his life until the public ministry. He knew something about the work of the farmer and the small shopkeeper. He was at home in the out-of-doors, loving flowers, birds, and all nature. He had been inside the one-roomed hut of the peasant who had to burn a candle or lamp to find a coin that had rolled from her hand. He knew something about the tradesmen and the fishermen, and he probably had among his friends other peasants who counted their sheep at night to be sure all were in the fold.

Jesus was a keen observer of life. Apparently he made friends easily and quickly and knew how to find at once a common ground of interest, no matter to whom he was talking. He loved people and could not bear to see any person using his life in opposition to the will of God.

THE BEGINNING OF THE PUBLIC MINISTRY

The Baptism of Jesus

From the earliest times Christianity dated its beginning with John the Baptist. The Gospel of Mark begins with the ministry of John and its first event is the baptism of Jesus by John the Baptist. Matthew, Luke, and John all relate the story of the baptism of Jesus, and apparently it was the act which introduced his public career.

The baptism occurred in the river Jordan, in the "wilderness" where John had established his headquarters. The baptism itself was the seal of God's approval upon the work that Jesus was doing. Jesus later gave eloquent testimony to John and expressed his approval of John's ministry. Jesus had found in John a prophetic religious leader, and for him baptism was a dedication to the kingdom of God.

The Temptation

After the baptism, Jesus was led by the Spirit to a desolate place where he was severely tempted. The Father's announcement at his baptism, "This is my beloved Son," may have been addressed more to Jesus than to the crowd, telling him of the Messianic nature of his work.

At any rate, Jesus now knew he had the power to work miracles, and when he thought of the poverty and distress of his own people he was tempted to use that power for their material benefit. He repudiated the material, though, for the dominion of things spiritual. He was tempted, also, to use his Messianic office as a miracle-working agency, but he turned instead to the preaching of the gospel to win the allegiance of men. He was also tempted to use political means to fulfill his Messianic office. Had he yielded he would have been supported by the Zealots and all the followers of the Maccabees. Jesus refused to bow to the Prince of this World no matter what the gains might seem to be.

Whatever else may be said about the experience in the wilderness, it must have been the time when Jesus fixed clearly in his own mind the nature and purpose of his ministry, its function, and his destiny. It is from his resistance to temptation and his power over evil that we get courage and strength for noble living today.

THE EARLY MINISTRY IN JUDEA

The Gospels were not written as biographies of Jesus, and so it is impossible to state with absolute accuracy just where the ministry of Jesus began and the chronology of the many events in it. Usually it is said that the ministry covered about three years, but there are some scholars who would hold that it was much less than that.

The First Disciples

According to the Gospel of John, Jesus began his ministry in Judea. There Andrew and Peter began to follow Jesus. John also states that Jesus then left for Galilee, where he made disciples of Philip and Nathanael. The actual order in which these disciples were called is not important, nor is the exact chronology of the life of Christ. It is important to remember that here were men who found in Jesus the answer to their hopes, and that as they surrendered their lives to his control they became changed men.

The First Miracle

John also gives us the first miracle of Jesus, that at the wedding in Cana of Galilee (John 2:1-11). The miracle was called a "sign," and evidently helped to strengthen the faith of the disciples in Jesus as the Messiah.

According to John's Gospel, Jesus went on to Capernaum, then to Jerusalem for the Feast of the Passover. As we shall see in a later chapter, there are many differences between the accounts of these events in the four Gospels, but that is because they were not written as historical biographies at all, but to present Jesus as Savior, Lord, Messiah, and King.

THE EARLY GALILEAN MINISTRY

Much of the early ministry of Jesus was in Galilee and it appears that Capernaum served as the center of much of this activity. Here Jesus taught in the synagogues, in private homes, in the open country, or wherever he found listeners. The mere rumor that Jesus was in a house brought crowds thronging to the doors until there was no more room. When he stood by the seashore and taught them, the crowds became so large that he put out into a boat to avoid the pushing and the jostling; he left them and went across the lake to the other side, only to find other crowds.

Miracles

Jesus performed many miracles during this early period of his work. Probably only a few of those that occurred are recorded in the Gospels. A man suffering from some kind of paralysis was lowered from the roof of the house where Jesus was, and Jesus healed him. He healed so many and his popularity became so intense that people believed if they could only touch him they would be healed. His compassion for suffering humanity was boundless; his heart of love broke with the sight of so much pain and sorrow, so much grief and sickness, so much trouble, so much anguish. Wherever he went he helped people; he healed them, opened blind eyes, made the crippled to walk again, and inspired hope and faith.

His followers were a motley crowd. There were some of the devout who hoped that he would prove to be the Messiah, and there were publicans, sinners, and all other classes of people. Some followed out of curiosity, some out of sincerity. Out of this crowd came some who became faithful and devoted disciples of the Lord, while others doubted and some began their opposition.

Choice of the Twelve

From among his devoted followers Jesus selected twelve men whom he chose "that they might be with him and that he might send them forth to preach." The names are given in Mark: "Simon, whom he surnamed Peter; James the son of Zebedee and John the brother of James, whom he surnamed Boanerges, that is, sons of thunder; Andrew, and Philip, and Bartholomew, and Matthew, and Thomas, and James the son of Alpheus, and Thaddeus, and Simon the Cananaean [or, Zealot], and Judas Iscariot, who betrayed him" (Mark 3:16-19). These men became his closest companions and his most devoted disciples.

Sermon on the Mount

The central core of the teachings of Jesus is found in the Sermon on the Mount. It was given chiefly for the Twelve, but evidently a large crowd heard it also. We may not state for certain just where and under what circumstances it was given, but it stands today as the greatest code of ethics in the world.

Jesus came into conflict with many religious leaders because he refused to recognize the validity of the oral law. He held to the Law of Moses, but said that even that Law needed a greater emphasis on the inner attitude. He came to fill the old Law full with spiritual significance and meaning. Jesus was saying that the real sin is not in an overt act, seen by men, but in the inner attitude known only to God. We begin to murder when we hate, so merely refraining from bloodshed is not fulfilling the intent of the Law of Moses regarding murder. Volumes have been written on the Sermon on the Mount; all that can be done here is to recall that it is the center of the teachings of Jesus and is rooted in his understanding of God and of the will of God for all people. No mere outward conformity to religious ritual will suffice; a life controlled by an inner attitude of surrender to God's will is needed.

Evangelism in Galilee

This Galilean leader who spoke with such directness and fervor, such understanding of people and of God, was moving the whole countryside. The results may have been as varied as were the people who heard his message. Like the grain in the Parable of the Sower, some of the teachings were lost sooner or later, but out of the masses some few took the word into their hearts and lives.

Jesus took the Twelve with him on his evangelistic tours "through cities and villages preaching and bringing the good news of the kingdom of God" (Luke 8:1). Frequently Jesus took the Twelve apart from the crowds for special teaching and spiritual nurture, for rest and meditation.

The Twelve were with Jesus for some of the most impressive miracles that were performed during this period, and they heard the parables Jesus

used for teaching the multitudes. Some of the outstanding miracles were the healing of the servant
of the centurion, the raising of the widow's son at
Nain, quieting the storm on the lake, restoring to
life the daughter of Jairus, opening the eyes of the
blind man, and causing a dumb child to speak.
(See Luke 7:1-17; 8:22-25; 8:40-56; Mark 8:22-26;
9:14-29.)

Jesus sent the twelve disciples out on a preaching mission in this ministry in Galilee, emphasizing
that they were to go out with complete dependence
upon God and in haste. There was a note of urgen-
cy about their mission, and Jesus warned them that
their reception might not always be a friendly one.
(See Mark 6:8ff.)

THE CRISIS IN GALILEE

Popular Acclaim

Jesus gained immense popularity among the
masses of common people. Crowds followed wherever he went, and multitudes pressed in upon him
whenever he appeared in public. There were times
when it was almost impossible for him to find
enough privacy to get rest and sleep.

Conflict with Leaders

The popularity did not go so far as to include
many of the religious leaders. Jesus disagreed with
them at many points, chiefly on his insistence that
God was more concerned about meeting the total
needs of mankind than he was in having them carefully keep minute details of the Law. Some of this
may have been due to ignorance on their part, but

much of it was because of jealousy and fear for their positions.

So long as Jesus interested only the common people he did not have much opposition, but now that his success seemed to threaten their own security, the leaders became increasingly critical of Jesus, then openly and aggressively hostile. (See Matthew 12:9-14; Luke 11:37-54; 16:14-17; John 7:25-34.)

Will He Be King?

Another factor that brought the Galilean ministry to a crisis was the fickle multitude who composed the large following of Jesus. They had witnessed his healings and other miracles, and now they wanted to make him their king (John 6:15). Jesus had long ago decided, however, that his kingdom was not political but spiritual, and he refused to listen to their appeal. When they began to understand that he would not be their political leader, many were disappointed and turned away.

The Great Confession

To the disciples, and more especially to the Twelve, this must have been a moment of supreme testing. The crowds were thinning and the hostility of the leaders becoming more apparent. But when Jesus tested their faith, on a retreat for spiritual and physical rest into Caesarea Philippi, Peter led their answer with his famous confession, "You are the Christ, the Son of the living God" (Matt. 16:16). Not only was this a crisis for the Twelve, a final testing of their resolute purpose to follow Jesus, but it was for him a victorious vindication of the choice he had made in selecting them as his closest followers.

It is always a moment of crisis when any man, confronted with his own need of God and his personal sense of inadequacy, throws his faith on Jesus as the eternal Son of God, regardless of what historical facts may or may not be summoned for support. The great adventure in spiritual living begins when a man makes this confession, and all that happens after only vindicates it.

CLOSE OF THE GALILEAN MINISTRY

Preparation for the Cross

The shadow of the cross had fallen on the path of Jesus long before now, but from the time of the confession of Peter even the disciples could see suffering and tragedy ahead. They did not understand nor comprehend it, so Jesus gave even more time to teaching them the spiritual significance of the suffering that he knew was waiting at the end of the journey to Jerusalem. (See Matthew 17:22-23; Luke 18:31-34.)

Jesus taught them that all living is barren until it is lost in a worthy and eternal cause; he who literally loses himself in the spiritual values on which the kingdom of God has its foundations has found life on its greatest meaning. Did Jesus know, even then, that after so many centuries men would "survey the wondrous cross" on which he had died, and, confronted with such inexpressible sorrow and such limitless love, would still say, "[it] demands my soul, my life, my all"?

The Transfiguration

This unusual experience is recorded by all three Synoptic writers. As for John, someone has said that Jesus is a transfigured person all the way through his Gospel. (See Matthew 17:1-13; Mark 9:2-13; Luke 9:28-36.) It is doubtful if anyone can fully understand the full significance of this event, and certainly it cannot be explained by the usual rational processes. Whatever happened, at the very least it was some unusual spiritual experience designed to strengthen Peter, James, and John. Jesus knew full well the struggle they would have to keep faith when all their hopes and dreams would lie in broken ruins at their feet; he knew the bitter reality they would have to meet when their Master had gone and they had to support their allegiance with nothing but sheer faith in him. And so he fortified them against that day of weakness. The story as recorded is meager and lacking in details, but we know that in some manner Jesus opened their spiritual eyes and let them see something of what can happen when Jesus Christ becomes Lord of all mankind.

Last Days in Galilee

During the last weeks of the Galilean ministry there were other miracles and events of note, but only two incidents are mentioned here.

The first is the address Jesus gave his disciples on the meaning of true greatness (Mark 9:33-50; Matt. 18:1-14; Luke 9:46-48). On the road to Capernaum, where Jesus was going for a few days of retirement, the disciples fell into an argument about their positions and relationships in the new kingdom of Jesus. He told them that no favored ones among them would have ground for hope of promotion; that true greatness is the product of unselfish service. This is one of the outstanding teachings of Jesus. The hallmark of a true Christian is his humility and sincerity in serving his fellow men. The "social climber" has no place in the thinking of Jesus. Only those who forget themselves in loving service will be remembered as truly great.

Jesus refused to be swayed by any social pressure. Even when his own brothers talked with him (John 7:3-9), he placed the will of God above family or personal ties. In an earlier period they had thought he was out of his mind (Mark 3:21), and even now they did not have true faith in him. Yet they wanted him to go openly to Jerusalem and show himself publicly, but Jesus refused to go until he felt that his time had come.

THE PEREAN MINISTRY

It was probably the next spring when Jesus said good-by to Galilee and went again to Jerusalem to attend the Passover at which he was crucified. The period and activity of this journey to the Holy City is known as the Perean ministry. Sometime before Jesus left Galilee for the last time he went to Jerusalem and was there for the Feast of Tabernacles (John 7:1-8, 10-53) and for the Feast of Dedication (John 10:22-42).

The Miracles and Teachings

Luke is the one who gives most of the information we have regarding the ministry in Perea. He mentioned the healing of the woman on the Sabbath, and the healing of the ten lepers (13:10-17; 17:11-19). Luke gives almost ten entire chapters to this phase of the ministry of Jesus, while none of the other writers mention it so specifically. (See Luke 9:51-19:28.)

As belonging to this period Luke records these immortal stories, the Rich Man and Lazarus, the Unjust Steward, the Pounds, the Lost Sheep, the Lost Coin, and the Lost Son, or the Prodigal Son. Jesus is fully aware of the growing opposition and of Herod's threat against his life and uses the time to prepare his disciples for the future events so that they will carry on after he has left them. It was probably about this time that the seventy were sent out.

A Steadfast Face

There is something magnificently courageous about the picture of Jesus Luke draws when he says that Jesus "steadfastly set his face to go to Jerusalem." Knowing full well what was waiting for him, he did not flinch nor shrink; he had settled all of this long ago and could now draw freely upon deep wells of strength and courage.

Raising of Lazarus

Probably to this same period belongs John's account of the death and raising of Lazarus (11:1-44). In a later chapter special attention will be given to the use which John makes of the miracles he records, but it should be noticed here that whatever happened at the tomb of Lazarus, Jesus surely was trying to teach his disciples that the grave could not hold him who had power over life and death. It must be remembered that Jesus used the miracles for their teaching values as well as for occasions to bring relief to suffering people.

Intimations of Death

In an earlier chapter it has been observed that no love was lost between the various religious groups of that day, but when Jesus appeared as a threat to all the religious leaders their concern for his overthrow became a matter of mutual interest. Sadducees, Pharisees, and the chief priests joined hands in cunning craftiness to plot against this man who moved so openly among them.

On the night before his triumphal entry into Jerusalem, according to the Gospel of John, Jesus was at the home of Mary, Martha, and Lazarus, and Mary anointed his feet with perfume. Judas raised a violent objection to the waste of valuable ointment, but Jesus quieted him by saying the poor would always be here and this act of devotion was an anointing for his burial.

How close the cross was coming to Jesus now! But how calm, how peaceful, how unperturbed was his spirit! The black shadow that grew darker by the hour served only to brighten the light of inner peace, strength, and harmony. While the halls of the great in Jerusalem were buzzing with the efforts to remove Jesus, he was quietly preparing his friends so they would not fail when the shock of his death struck them full in their hearts. Majestic splendor was there in the small circle of friends in the little house in Bethany that night. And surely He slept peacefully while the chief priests and the other religious leaders went slinking through the dark streets of Jerusalem, thickening their infamous plot against him.

Topics for Further Study

1. Was the life of Jesus perfect religiously from the very beginning? What did the neighbors of Jesus think about him?

2. Which would you say influenced Jesus most as he grew up in the village of Nazareth: books, the out-of-doors, people, his family, the teachings of the synagogue, or his friends?

3. The *Westminster Bible Atlas* and the *Westminster Bible Dictionary* will be helpful in gaining a clear idea of the geography of Palestine and of the country surrounding Nazareth.

4. Can you find anything in the New Testament which gives you reason to believe that Joseph died and left to Jesus the task of earning the living for the family? Who would do this when Jesus left home?

5. In a Bible dictionary look up the words *synagogue* and *rabbi*, to get clearer detail on the kind of church and school Jesus attended and the kind of teachers he had.

6. What besides religion was taught in the school Jesus attended?

7. Contrast the ministry of Jesus and that of John the Baptist, taking special notice of their messages, their places of work, the audiences they had, their attitudes toward people.

8. Jesus and John the Baptist lived at the same time, in the same country, under conditions very similar; how do you account for the differences in them and their messages?

9. From what you find in the four Gospels, can you trace the journeys of Jesus from Nazareth to Jerusalem? Where did he spend the most time? Why?

10. How many members of the Herodian family do you find referred to in the New Testament? Compare their place in history with that of Jesus and John the Baptist. What made the difference?

CHAPTER III

AN OUTLINE OF
THE LIFE OF JESUS

(continued)

THE ROAD TO JERUSALEM

Jesus had set his face like a flint to go to Jerusalem. The coming Feast of the Passover furnished the occasion for that final entry to the great city. The Passover was the greatest of all the Jewish feasts, and no loyal Jew would miss it if it were humanly possible for him to attend. Aside from the spiritual implications in the experience for him, Jesus realized the opportunity this event would give him to proclaim himself to the multitude who would gather in Jerusalem from all over Palestine. Peasants from Galilee and powerful leaders among the Sadducees and Pharisees would all be gathered into the Holy City, In a sense more profound than any of the people could ever know, the "Lamb of God" was being prepared for the sacrificial offering.

Once more Jesus visited Capernaum before

going to Jerusalem. As he and the disciples walked along the dusty road, Jesus heard their arguments about greatness in his kingdom. It was on this trip that he took a little child and placed him in their midst and taught them the true meaning of service and of greatness. It is a lesson our world still needs, a lesson every follower of Jesus today must learn for himself.

From Capernaum Jesus went through Perea on his road to Jerusalem. As they neared Jerusalem the band of followers with their Master passed through Jericho. Here Jesus ministered to the needs of Zaccheus, another tax collector, rich and corrupt and unscrupulous. On this Jericho road was Bartimeus, the blind man whose insistent and courageous faith brought healing and hope from Jesus.

ENTRY INTO JERUSALEM

Near Bethany Jesus paused for rest, while two of his followers were sent into the town to secure a young ass which Jesus said they would find in a certain place. We are not told who owned this animal or the owner's relation to Jesus; we simply know that some preparation had been made for Jesus to borrow the animal.

But why use the ass? Jesus and his disciples had been walking for many days; why should this last short trip to Jerusalem not also be made on foot? And why did Jesus send two men to get the ass, when he might easily have gone after it himself? It appears that Jesus intended now to demonstrate to all the Jews that he was their Messiah, by riding into the city as a king. Until now he had not proclaimed his Messiahship very widely; the time had arrived for him to announce it both by word of mouth and by this more dramatic and graphic presentation.

Enter the King!

A king would ride into his capital city on a charging horse, a prancing war horse appropriately decorated. Jesus rode in upon a humble beast, an ass. This was in keeping with the tradition of Jewish kings, for Saul, David, and Solomon had ridden upon asses. This animal was also the symbol of peace, while a horse was symbolic of war. Furthermore, the Jewish people expected that their king would enter Jerusalem riding upon an ass.

We are told that the crowds which thronged the roadsides tore branches from the trees and threw their garments into the street to make a carpet upon which Jesus would ride. Their songs resounded throughout the city, "Hosannah to our King; Blessed is he that cometh in the name of the Lord." But it was a fickle crowd. Their enthusiastic reception turned to sullen and bitter hatred almost overnight. The voices shouting "Hosannah" today were crying lustily, "Let him be crucified," in less than a week.

Jesus did nothing either to encourage the people in this welcome to Jerusalem or to prevent their demonstrations. He simply accepted what was given. He had often stated that he was not the kind of Messiah he knew the Jews were expecting, but for this one occasion he did accept their praise and adulation. Centuries later our minds go back to this joyous reception, when once a year we observe Palm Sunday in whatever ways we think are most appropriate. Do we as quickly reverse our attitudes now as did the Jews then?

An Evening in Bethany

Jesus went on to the Temple, the center of all religious life for the Jews, but he did not remain there long. He accepted the praise of the crowds and then joyful acclaim of the children. He left quietly, then, to spend the night with his friends in Bethany—Mary, Martha, and Lazarus. Their home was always his home when he was in the city; how much must he have appreciated their generous hospitality, the peaceful quietness, the understanding warmth of their home on this occasion! Have you ever thought what home Jesus would choose for his retreat each night if the week in Jerusalem were to be repeated in your own town? What family would supply the undergirding strength of understanding and quiet confidence, the friendship that shares every burden and every care without prying questions?

CONFLICT WITH JEWISH RULERS

Through all his ministry until now, Jesus had not sought clashes with the Jewish leaders. He took their insults without a word. Now he throws caution to the winds. His accusations of hypocrisy and disloyalty are hurled straight and fast. They brought a response from the rulers at once.

Cleansing the Temple

On a day early in this week Jesus entered the Temple, saw the salesmen who had doves to sell the worshiping Jews and the money-changers who would change the coin of the Empire into the Temple coin. All of them were in the business for profit. The common folk who came there to worship were being exploited by the greedy officials. The rulers of the Jews knew and approved all this commercial traffic that went on right under their very eyes, but Jesus did not. He made a whip out of cords or rope and drove out the salesmen and money-changers, overthrowing all their tables.

We do not know as much as we would like to about this act of Jesus. Some people have seen in it a justification of the use of force. Others have gone to great lengths to show that it was not force at all. We do know it must have been a very important thing to Jesus, for it occupied a prominent place in this last visit to Jerusalem. And whatever it tells us about the kind of person Jesus was must harmonize with everything else that we know about him.

Jesus was not attacking individuals as such here so much as he was trying to show that the leaders had obscured the meaning of true religion with greed and selfishness. The Temple was built as a house of prayer, but these men cared little about prayer. Every Jew was required by law to make a sacrifice of some kind; even the poorest Jew must sacrifice at least a pair of doves, and wealthier persons were required to sacrifice something more expensive. These who commercialized the Temple were selling the doves at exorbitant rates and, as we have seen, were charging high fees for changing money; they were literally robbing the poor people in their very act of worship. They were making a "den of thieves" out of the Temple. Small wonder Jesus drove them out. Whether he used a whip or not, his act needs no justification or explanation; it stands on its own—blazing and divine justice overwhelmed at the degradation and greed which can underlie a pious act in the name of religion.

Attempts to Trap Jesus

Day by day Jesus came to the Temple to continue his teaching of the people under the watchful eyes of the rulers who were scheming and plotting to trap him and put him to death. Each night he returned to the quiet home in Bethany, where prayer and friends and the quiet renewal of inner resources fortified him for the hours just ahead.

Cleansing the Temple had turned the religious leaders against Jesus. If there had been any question about their stand before, his open and sharp criticism of them now made them bloodthirsty. He charged them with trying to cover up their unfair and unjust treatment of the common people with a cloak of religion. They tried to trap him into a denial of loyalty to Caesar, which could have brought him before the civil authorities for trial, but he deftly turned their question with the words we know so well, "Render therefore to Caesar the things that are Caesar's; and to God the things that are God's" (Matt. 22:21). They tried to trap him in hypothetical questions about the judgment and the resurrection, but they were no match for Jesus. They tried again on the Law itself, only to get the reply: "You shall love the Lord your God with all your heart, and with all your soul, and with all your mind. This is the great and first commandment. And a second is like it, You shall love your neighbor as yourself. On these two commandments depend all the law and the prophets" (22:37-40). Matthew sums up their baffled confusion thus: "And no one was able to answer him a word, nor from that day did any one dare to ask him any more questions" (22:45).

Matthew follows this with the denunciation of the scribes and Pharisees and with the seven "woes" Jesus pronounced upon them. The justice and the mercy of God, the "goodness and the severity" of God, are shown in bold relief when the "woes" against the Pharisees are followed by words of tender lament as Jesus looked at Jerusalem, the city of such profound possibilities, and wept over it.

Mounting Tension

Day by day the tension with the rulers mounted. Everything Jesus said and did seemed to irritate them and fill them with envy and jealousy. In these days occurred such interesting happenings as the cursing of the fig tree, a symbol of the barren and unfruitful Jewish nation, the blessing upon the widow who gave her small offering of two mites, the teachings about the wise and foolish maidens, the story of the talents, and the picture of the surprises of the last judgment. They were days filled with much more than we find recorded in the Gospels, but even what we find there would make them busy and eventful days.

Darker grew the shadow, and shorter. Jesus knew that while he was meeting daily in the Temple with all who would listen, somewhere in Jerusalem there lay two rough, heavy poles, and somewhere in that city were the nails, only a dozen or so, that would pierce his hands. These were days of sifting, of testing, of separation; the final test was only a few hours away.

THE STORM CLOUDS DARKEN

Nothing is known of how Jesus spent Wednesday of this eventful week. It probably was spent in quiet prayer and meditation in the hallowed seclusion of the Bethany home, but we cannot say with certainty.

The Passover

Thursday evening was the time appointed for the observance of the Feast of the Passover, when every Jew would participate in this memorial of God's deliverance of the children of Israel. Jesus went with his followers to the guest chamber, or the "upper room" in the home of one of his friends in Jerusalem. Jesus evidently had made some advance preparation, for two of the disciples were instructed to go into the city and to follow the first man they met carrying a pitcher of water. Jesus told them this man would lead them to the place where the Paschal lamb was to be prepared for the Passover Supper. Here the Son of God partook with his disciples of the Passover lamb; then he tried again to tell them that he was the Lamb of God, "slain from the foundation of the world."

Treasures of the Upper Room

The dark clouds were gathering, and the fury of the storm would be unleashed in a few short hours, but here in the upper room quiet peace reigned supreme. For those last hours together Jesus reserved some of the truly lasting and most wonderful teachings and experiences of his entire ministry. John gives us those profound teachings of Jesus in chapters 13 to 18 of his Gospel, where are found the admonition to humble service, the assurance of a reunion in the Father's house, the promise of greater works and of the gift of the Holy Spirit, the Parable of the Vine and the Branches, and the immortal prayer sometimes called the "High-Priestly Prayer" of Jesus.

Servant and Lord

Here in the last moments of friendship, when the essence of a loving fellowship was being pressed out by time, Jesus gave two simple demonstrations or visual portrayals of the two great basic truths of his kingdom. They had to do with relationships. One is vertical—the relationship of the disciples and God through Jesus Christ. The other is a horizontal relationship—the attitude and action the followers of Christ express toward each other.

The latter Jesus illustrated by girding himself with a towel and in the manner of a humble household servant washing the feet of the disciples. Peter remonstrated, but when he saw the full significance of the act became more than willing. In one simple but profound act, Jesus showed the disciples what he had meant when he said, "He that would be greatest among you, let him be the servant of all." That attitude of kindly service toward each other needs to possess the twentieth-century followers of Jesus, for true greatness still lies in humble unassuming service to one's fellow men.

Our relationship to God was graphically illustrated by the bread and the wine. Jesus had finished the Passover feast, and now he began what we call the Lord's Supper. It was a dramatic presentation of the truth that we keep our right relationship with God only as we partake of the grace and redeeming love of Christ. As we are united to him we become united to each other—"one bread and one body." How sorely did those disciples need these two great truths to come alive for them, and how great is our need today that these fundamental truths of our faith become living and vibrant factors in our own lives!

Judas the Betrayer

Two days before this the rulers were puzzling how to trap Jesus and put him to death without at the same time bringing down the wrath of the people or the scorn of the Romans upon their own heads.

The matter was serious, for Jesus adroitly evaded the traps they set for him each day. Then Judas solved the problem. Judas was a disciple, and he would betray his Master for a small fee! Why Judas turned on Jesus is a matter of speculation, and one guess may be quite as good as another. Some think Judas wanted to force Jesus to manifest his power and thus usher in the new kingdom. Others think he had lost all hope of the Messiahship of Jesus, and in a despairing moment of utter dissillusionment sold out to the Jewish leaders. Whatever the motives or reasons, we do know that Judas betrayed his Lord and then regretted it bitterly.

Among those few who were faithful to the last, among these who had stood the tests of popularity and of persecution, stood Judas the betrayer. Jesus knew Judas had sold him for a paltry thirty pieces of silver and even recalled the action to Judas at the table. If Judas wept bitterly and in complete and utter self-condemnation hanged himself, can we imagine the sorrow and acute disappointment that tore at the heart of Jesus? Judas, whom He had trusted, Judas whom He had chosen and called. Judas reached with Jesus into the common bowl of food, and perhaps as their eyes met across the table, Jesus resigned himself to the final decision of his one-time friend: "What thou doest, do quickly."

In Gethsemane

Judas had slipped away into the darkness with his troubled conscience and the haunting memory of the face of Jesus to go with him to the galling end of his chosen road. The eleven other disciples seized the occasion to pledge anew their undying loyalty to Jesus; then the little band of twelve sang a hymn and walked out into the future. Across the brook Kidron to the Mount of Olives they went, to a secluded garden called Gethsemane. Perhaps the Master and these followers had been here before for prayer; we do not know.

Jesus took Peter, James, and John apart from the others and asked them to wait while he went a little farther to pray. There near the top of the Mount of Olives, beneath the Paschal moon, in the rock-strewn garden with its gnarled and twisted old olive trees, Jesus faced his last major battle. Is it not probable that he let his mind turn back the pages of his ministry, perhaps going back to the earliest events of his earthly life? One by one he reviewed the occasions when he had come to a major decision. Perhaps he paused a long time at the page on which he had recorded the lonely, agonizing days in the wilderness at the beginning of his ministry. Doubtless hundreds of faces flashed before him there that night: faces of friends, tried and true; faces of the people to whose dire needs he had ministered—the hungry, tired, weary, sick, blind, lame; faces of the Jewish leaders, smug with satisfaction at their success in overlaying religion with their selfish ways; the face of Judas; the face of Mary, his mother; these to whom through the years he had imparted the inner secret of his heart. Maybe he prayed for them. Perhaps the memory of all the multitudes he had seen stayed with him there, these thousands upon thousands who had neither bread nor money, friend nor religious guide; these sheep milling about on the barren plateaus without any shepherd to care.

"Nevertheless . . ."

We do know that there Jesus prayed. The burden of a lost world pressed in upon him. Was death the only way out for him? Was it the best way out? Would the kingdom of love really conquer the kingdom of darkness? Would his dying make any impact upon the deeply entrenched wrongs he found in his day? Death stalked up behind him as he knelt in prayer and leered at him from behind every olive tree and lurking shadow. All the greed and hate and envy, all the sin and selfishness, all the iniquity of the world gathered there to wrestle with the Son of God.

The three disciples had pledged their loyalty, but now that Jesus needed them most they were asleep. We can only dimly guess at all Jesus meant as he cried out in lonely despair, "If it be possible let this cup pass from me." But he went beyond that intensely human petition to the victory of surrender to God's will, "Nevertheless, not my will, but thine be done." Once having fought it through in his own soul, Jesus could rise with confidence and face the end with a courage born of answered prayer. Perhaps the prayer was not answered the way he wanted it answered, but for him it was enough to know that the Father had heard, the Father's will was being done, and the Father would triumph over sin and unrighteousness.

The Betrayal

Jesus roused his sleepy followers and with them went out to meet the enemy. The voices of the soldiers, the sound of their footsteps on the loose gravel, the clang of their swords, must have floated up to Jesus, and he could surely see their torches as they wound up the hillside, eerie shadows reminding him of his recent struggle with the hosts of darkness.

Judas stepped out from the band of soldiers, a few Romans who probably made up the night watch of the Temple guard. Judas had arranged a signal by which the soldiers should know Jesus—a kiss. What pain must have shot through the heart of Jesus as he felt that cold kiss of disloyalty and betrayal.

Peter reached for his sword at once. Peter, who had always meant so well, but who blundered so often, he would not stand idly by and see his Master taken. Gently Jesus reprimanded Peter, and the sound of rattling swords drifted down the hillside

as Jesus quietly reminded the soldiers that he had
been in the Temple daily unarmed and unharmful.

THE ARREST AND TRIAL

The soldiers roughly seized Jesus and dragged
him down into the city. All the disciples fled then—
these whose presence would have spoken so elo-
quently of loyalty and faithfulness. Peter sneaked
along behind at a safe distance—he "followed afar
off."

To the palace of the high priest Jesus was led.
Caiaphas was the high priest in name, but the real
"power behind the throne" was his father-in-law,
Annas, who had formerly been the high priest.
Annas controlled the Temple in all financial poli-
cies, so was the one who stood to lose most when
Jesus drove out the money-changers. Jesus was a
threat to all the power and security of Annas and
Caiaphas and all their lesser satellites. Jesus must
be put out of the way.

Much as Annas and Caiaphas wanted to be rid
of Jesus, they certainly did not want any public
knowledge of their own connection with that action. Furthermore, a trial in the daytime would
have to be more just than the farce they had
planned. Mark implies that the Sanhedrin was
called into special session during the night for a
hearing of Jesus at the palace of the high priest. At
this night meeting Jesus was accused and condemned, illegal though the whole prodecure was.
Two questions were put to Jesus in the hearing before Annas. First, Jesus was asked whether he was
the Christ, the Messiah, and then whether he was
the Son of God. The answer Jesus gave to both
questions was enough for these evil plotters to as-

sume that Jesus had confessed to the crimes which would be charged against him. He was led then to the palace of Caiaphas, and then early in the morning to the home of the Roman governor, Pilate.

The Charges Against Jesus

At the trial before Pilate these charges were made against Jesus. First, Jesus was turning the Jewish nation away from its heritage and the principles on which it was founded. Second, he had told his followers they should not pay tribute to Caesar. Third, Jesus claimed to be a king, or the Messiah. Of these three, apparently only the third held any interest for Pilate, and the answer Jesus gave to this charge seemed to satisfy Pilate that he was innocent of all three charges. Pilate told the priests and the crowd that had gathered that he found no reason for condemning Jesus.

Jesus Before Roman Authorities

It was illegal for the Jews to hold a trial on the day just before the Sabbath or on any sacred feast day, such as the Passover. It was also against their law to condemn a person at the same trial in which his case was heard. Apparently they had hoped to escape blame on both of these counts by letting Pilate handle their crooked proceedings. Pilate, on the other hand, seemed to have no desire at all to carry any blame which he could clearly see belonged to the high priest and elders of the people. So when Pilate's announcement of the innocency of Jesus served only to further anger the Jewish leaders, he thought of a way out that would relieve him of responsibility and still satisfy the priests. Pilate would send Jesus to Herod. Jesus was a Galilean, and Herod was tetrarch over Galilee, but happened to be visiting in Jerusalem at this time. To Herod Jesus was sent!

The plot was short-lived. Herod might have held some mild curiosity about Jesus, but to all his questions the Master was silent. So in a short while Jesus was back in Pilate's hall of judgment, this time to be robed in purple, crowned with thorns, and mocked as "King of the Jews."

Pilate called the chief priests together again. It would be natural that by this time a fairly large crowd would have gathered, as the news went from one to another. Pilate still had no just cause to crucify Jesus, but he was willing to have Jesus scourged, reprimanded severely, and released. None of that for the priests! When Pilate suggested that Jesus be the prisoner who would be released on the Feast of the Passover, he was utterly defeated. The proposal was in line with the custom of the Roman governor of Jerusalem to release one of his Jewish prisoners on the Passover, more as a gesture of generosity and an effort to secure popular good will than for any other reason.

Barabbas or Jesus?

The priests were undoubtedly well distributed in the crowd, and led the people in crying down Pilate's offer to release Jesus. They wanted Barabbas! Now Barabbas was being held on a murder charge and on further charges of trying to lead a riot against Rome. He it was whose bands were cut and who stumbled out to freedom, while Jesus of Nazareth took the place not only of Barabbas but of all mankind. The crowd, urged on by their priestly leaders, cried louder and louder to crucify Jesus, and Pilate yielded.

Pilate's sense of justice would not let Jesus go without one more protest, so Pilate publicly and literally washed his hands of all responsibility, and the Jewish leaders gladly assumed it. But neither Pilate nor any other man can wash his hands of this Son of God. Jesus is not so easily disposed of as that!

THE CRUCIFIXION

The Romans crucified their criminals in some spot of prominence, where all who passed by would be reminded of the justice and severity of the Roman law. The Jews, also, had a law of their own which required that a crucifixion or other execution could not occur in the city. The place chosen for Jesus was a small hill called Golgotha, just outside Jerusalem.

When Pilate yielded to the pressure of the officials, Jesus was again mocked and shamefully mistreated by the soldiers in charge. They tossed a purple robe over him in derision of his claim to be a king. His crown was of branches of a thorn tree. He was forced to carry his own cross, like a common criminal, to the place of his execution. Once, when he faltered beneath its heavy weight, a certain Simon of Cyrene was forced by the soldiers to help Jesus carry the cross.

A sign which the soldiers nailed to the cross read, "King of the Jews." The chief priests immediately protested that Jesus was not their king, but Pilate held his ground this time and the sign remained. There has been much speculation about the exact manner in which Jesus was crucified. We know that he was nailed to the cross, and that just before sundown the centurion in charge ordered a soldier to pierce the side of Jesus with a spear.

Who Was at the Cross?

Volumes have been written about the people Jesus saw from the cross. Some writers have estimated that the crowd who saw Jesus die would run into the hundreds of thousands, while others give a much more conservative estimate.

Peter had denied his Lord the night before when Jesus was being tried before Annas, but surely Peter was not far away now when the end of the earthly life of Jesus was so near at hand. John was there, and to him Jesus commended Mary for care and keeping. Beside Mary the mother of Jesus were her sister and Mary Magdalene. The fact that the other followers are not mentioned by name does not necessarily prove that they were not near the cross.

The soldiers and their centurion were there. The soldiers threw their dice to see who would get the robe of Jesus. The centurion saw everything, and gave the verdict of all history, "Surely this was the Son of God."

The two thieves were there—one on either side of Jesus. One recognized in Jesus a Savior and repented and called for forgiveness in his last hours on the cross. Jesus assured him of forgiving love. The other thief had eyes to see, but saw only another man dying on a cross.

The scribes and elders and chief priests were there. They mocked him, "He saved others; he cannot save himself." It must be remembered that these leaders were the ones who carried responsibility for the crucifixion of Jesus—not the masses of the Jews. It was men like Annas and Caiaphas who beyond all doubt really knew that Jesus was the Son of God, but whose deep-seated love for power and fame and position drove them to the despicable position of being crucifiers of Jesus.

The Last Words

Jesus saw Mary, his mother, standing near the cross, and John, his disciple. To his mother he said, "Woman, behold your son," and to John, "Behold your mother." With these words he commended Mary to the loving care of John.

Once he called out, "I thirst," and he was brought some wine mixed with myrrh, such as that usually given to criminals to lessen their pain (John 19:29-30). His reply to the thief who called for help has already been observed, "Truly, I say to you, today will you be with me in paradise" (Luke 23:43).

The most despairing cry of all are the words, "My God, my God, why hast thou forsaken me?" We stand in subdued awe before those words, for they dimly hint of an experience through which Jesus passed which is beyond our poor power to imagine or comprehend. We can only bow ōur hearts in humble thanksgiving that when Jesus faced that last long walk in the darkness, alone, he did not shrink, but carried the victory to the end.

Sometimes criminals died a slow, torturous death on the cross. It was not unusual for them to linger as much as two or three days. To hasten death, the soldiers would break the legs of the condemned. This they were going to do to Jesus, but when the soldier saw he was already dead he did not break the bones. Jesus had died with the lips, "Father, into thy hands I commend my spirit," and "It is finished."

THE BURIAL

The Jews would not permit the body of a criminal to remain unburied after sunset, so something had to be done about the body of Jesus. His own disciples seem to have vanished from the earth at this time, for they are not mentioned. Rather, it was two men of high position and influence who came to take down the body and make arrangements for having it prepared for burial. These men were Nicodemus, who had visited Jesus by night, and Joseph of Arimathea. Joseph went to Pilate and requested permission to bury the body of Jesus and was granted that privilege.

Tenderly these two men, along with the women who had stayed loyally by to the end, removed the body from the cross and prepared it for burial. They then wrapped it in a shroud and placed it in a tomb in a garden near by, a tomb Joseph had prepared for his own family use against that day when death should claim one of his loved ones. A rock was dragged against the entrance to the tomb.

What long thoughts must have passed through the minds of all those who so carefully ministered these last gestures of loving tenderness! What did Mary think as she finally turned away from the tomb and in the gathering shadows of twilight trudged wearily back to an empty house? What did Nicodemus think as he looked through his tears at the still form of this man who had searched his own heart and with penetrating skill had laid bare the emptiness of one who has not been born of the

Spirit? What did the Roman guards think, as they reviewed the unsual events of the afternoon—the thunder and lightning and the darkening of the sun itself? What did Annas and Caiaphas think as they finally lay down to sleep that night, each alone with his conscience, recalling the face of Jesus as he had looked at them through the torturous pain, remembering their own consternation at finding the veil of the Temple torn from top to bottom? Alone with their own sober thoughts, the disciples tossed restlessly through the long, slow night, confused and wondering about this One who had saved others but who had not saved himself.

THE RESURRECTION

The women who had hastily prepared the body of Jesus for burial so that it could be placed in the tomb before sundown Friday evening, could not return to complete their task on the following day, for it was the Sabbath. But early on the first day of the week they returned to the tomb of Jesus to finish the burial rites. The tomb was empty! Jesus was not there! When an angel of the Lord said to them, "He is not here, for he is risen as he said; go tell his disciples and Peter," they ran to tell the disciples the news. Peter and John rushed back to the tomb to confirm the story, but an empty tomb was not sufficient to convince them.

Mary Magdalene, in utter despair, through her tears and her sobs cried out to one who she thought was a gardener that the body had been removed. But the "gardener" called her by name, and in an indescribably joyous recognition, Mary knelt before him, able to say only, "Rabboni!" (which means Teacher).

Thus it was that the disciples discovered for themselves that Jesus was alive again. They saw him, talked with him, ate with him, worshiped him. For those who, for all time, were in the best position to verify the facts, there was no doubt that Jesus the Christ was alive and victorious over death and the grave. Through the centuries there have been many who have sought a rationale for the resurrection of Jesus; for those to whom he has come as a living, powerful, loving Savior, there is no doubt.

THE ASCENSION

Not much is told us of the forty days Jesus was upon the earth after the resurrection, nor is there much said about the ascension. Both are treated as historical events which need no explanation. History never has to be *explained;* it is the theoretical which calls for explanation, while fact stands on its own.

We know that "Jesus did many other signs in the presence of the disciples, which are not written in this book" (John 20:30) and that one day "he was lifted up, and a cloud took him out of their sight" (Acts 1:9). We know, too, the glory of his presence in our own lives here and now, and the power of his resurrection in giving victory over all sin and death itself to each one who humbly follows all the way.

We know beyond all shadow of doubt that "God so loved the world that he gave his only Son, that whoever believes in him should not perish but have eternal life. For God sent the Son into the world, not to condemn the world, but that the world might be saved through him" (John 3:16-17).

TOPICS FOR FURTHER THOUGHT

1. In the day in which Jesus lived, which was more important: the teachings of Jesus or his ministry of healing and helpfulness in other ways? Which has made the more lasting impression in history?

2. What reasons can you assign to the fact that the ministry of Jesus was so closely confined to the Jews, especially in view of the universality of his teachings?

3. From what you find in the Gospels, what did each of the twelve disciples probably think of Jesus?

4. If Jesus knew what was in the heart of Judas, how do you account for the fact that Jesus never dismissed him from the company of the Twelve? If Judas could not be trusted at all, why did Jesus entrust him with money?

5. On what basis did Jesus decide whether anything in the Jewish Law was to be observed or not?

6. What tests did Jesus use to determine the will of God?

7. If you could assign only one chief reason for the crucifixion of Jesus, what would it be?

8. Is it likely that Caiaphas or Annas or other Jewish leaders really knew that Jesus was the Christ, the Son of God?

9. How did the transfiguration experience strengthen the disciples?

10. Did the Messiah idea ever appeal to Jesus as it did to some of his followers? Do you think Jesus ever thought his work would die out if he were crucified?

CHAPTER IV

FOUR BOOKS, ONE STORY

Our sources for the life and teachings of Jesus are the four Gospels, Matthew, Mark, Luke, and John. All four of these books together give us the gospel, the good news, the story of full salvation for all men everywhere. Yet no one of these books agrees in complete detail with any of the others. There are marked differences between all four books. In this chapter we shall examine these books, try to discover how and why they differ in their accounts of the life of Jesus, and try to find how all four of them fit together into one story.

A statement from the Gospel of John is pertinent here: "Now Jesus did many other signs in the presence of the disciples, which are not written in this book; but these are written that you may believe that Jesus is the Christ, the Son of God, and that believing you may have life in his name" (John 20:30-31). John tells us clearly that he has an evangelistic purpose in writing his book. He was writing for a verdict; he was writing for decisions. The same might be said of the writers of the other books also. They were not writing biographies; they were telling the wonderful story of the Son of God who had come to earth to save men from their sins; they were telling the most breathtaking news the world had ever heard, and they wanted to tell it convincingly and with fervor. They were not writing history as such; they were proclaiming a message.

Any four people today who should tell about the same event or the same person would each tell the story somewhat differently. Each person would tell that part of the story which made the greatest impression upon him or which he wanted to tell for the effect it might have upon others. Thus all four such persons might truthfully describe such an event and yet all four stories be different. So it was with the writers of the four Gospels. With all their differences, all four Gospels are true. Each writer had his own audience and his own specific purpose, and under divine guidance he selected those parts of the story of Jesus which to him were most important and would help his readers to believe on Jesus as their Savior.

THE GOSPEL OF MATTHEW

It has been said that the most important book ever written is the Gospel of Matthew. That may be an overstatement, yet Matthew's Gospel certainly is one of the important books of the New Testament and especially helpful in any study of the life and teachings of Jesus. Here are a few reasons why it is outstanding in this respect:

1. Matthew is more orderly in its arrangement and more systematic in its presentation than any of

the other Gospels. The outline of the book is easy to follow; for example, five major divisions with a prologue and an epilogue are plainly discernible.

2. In this book the teachings of Jesus are presented much more systematically than in any other of the Gospels. It is also the fullest and most complete single record we have of the teachings of Jesus.

3. All the way through this book the writer keeps much closer to the Jewish setting of the life of Jesus than does any other writer.

4. This book is pre-eminently a Gospel for use in showing the life and teachings of Jesus to the church. It is placed first in our New Testament, not because it was written first, but because it was the most important Gospel in the early church.

5. Matthew is careful to give an accurate account of the religious significance of Jesus. He is not presented as a philosopher or as simply another prophet, but as a teacher and as one who lived out the religious implications of his teachings—the Son of God, the Messiah-King.

6. Better than any other Gospel Matthew links together the Old and the New Testaments. The writer presents Jesus as one who has come not to destroy the Law, but to fill the old form fuller of spiritual content and meaning than it ever had been before.

Purpose of Matthew

It is the apparent purpose of Matthew to prove to the Jews that Jesus is the promised Messiah and their true king. One way that he attempts to do this is through his frequent use of Old Testament prophecy. He always uses prophecies that are both typical and specific, however, as he shows how Jesus is the true fulfillment of prophecy. Consider these examples: Jesus is born of a virgin as the prophet foretold (1:22-23); the birth of Jesus in Bethlehem is considered the fulfillment of prophecy (2:5-6); the flight of Joseph, Mary, and the baby into the land of Egypt (2:14-15); after the return from Egypt, the establishing of the residence of Joseph in Nazareth (2:23); the departure from Nazareth and the residence in Capernaum (4:13-16); the entire ministry of healing the sick and casting out of evil spirits (8:16-17); the reluctance with which Jesus met the acclaim of the crowds (12:15-21); the manner in which Jesus taught in parables (13:34-35); the manner in which Jesus came into Jerusalem at the triumphal entry (21:1-5); the purchase of the potter's field with the money given Judas for the betrayal (27:6-10). None of the other writers use prophecy in the same way in which Matthew does.

Only Matthew and Luke give the genealogies, and they are not identical! There are several explanations offered for these differences. One explanation is that Matthew is trying to show the Jews that Jesus is their king and the Messiah, so he traces the ancestry of Jesus back through the legal heirs of the throne of David, while Luke uses other names to follow a more prophetic genealogy. Matthew's concern to portray the Jewish Messiah is perhaps the reason for going back to Abraham in his genealogy, whereas Luke goes back to Adam, in order to portray Jesus as the universal Savior.

Differences in Birth Stories

Mark and John give none of the nativity stories, nor do they give any information about the boyhood of Jesus. Matthew alone of the four writers gives the story of the slaughter of the infants by Herod the Great, and only he tells of the flight into Egypt. Only Matthew tells of the visit of the Wise Men, but he omits entirely any reference to the announcement of the angels to the shepherds and of the visit of the shepherds to Bethlehem. Matthew says nothing at all about the boyhood of Jesus. After recording the return to Nazareth from Egypt, Matthew abruptly begins the story of the public ministry of Jesus with the baptism by John (3:13-17). Luke also gives the baptism of Jesus (3:21-22), while both Mark and John begin with references to the meeting of Jesus and John, in their first chapters.

Work of John the Baptist

The ministry of John the Baptist and the baptism of Jesus must have been considered important by all the Gospel writers, for all four of them refer to both. Matthew goes into some detail to give the setting for the work of John the Baptist and something of the content of his message. Matthew also tells more in detail about the baptism of Jesus than do the other writers. The Gospel of John, in fact, refers to the baptism of Jesus as having taken place, but does not give any of the description of the event.

There is very little difference between the accounts of the temptation of Jesus in the wilderness in the Gospel of Matthew and the Gospel of Luke.

John makes no mention at all of the wilderness experience, and Mark disposes of it in two brief sentences. Matthew and Mark both connect the close of the temptation and the return to Galilee with the arrest of John the Baptist, while Luke simply states that Jesus returned to Galilee and makes no mention of John the Baptist in connection with it. Luke does tell of the arrest of John the Baptist, but brings it into his narrative much earlier than this.

The Sermon on the Mount

In Matthew three entire chapters are given to the Sermon on the Mount, which is not reported as such in either Mark or John, and which is taken care of in separate passages in Luke. Both Matthew and Luke report this discourse as taking place rather early in the public career of Jesus. In Matthew, where the author is trying to show Jesus as the king, a strong emphasis is placed upon the standards of the new kingdom. The Kingdom of which Jesus is the head is not an earthly kingdom, but is the reign of God in the hearts of men. The Zealots believed that the coming of the Kingdom depended upon the activity and initiative of men. They insisted that the Jews should revolt against the Romans, and that the Kingdom would come when they should be successful in such a rebellion. The Pharisees, on the other hand, believed that God would bring in the Kingdom when the people were ready for it, and that readiness consisted entirely in the strict observance of the Law. Contrast both of these teachings with that of Jesus as recorded by Matthew in the Sermon on the Mount, where the true kingdom of God comes whenever and wherever an individual opens his heart and life to accept and do the will of God. A new order, a spiritual order, comes into being as individual lives are changed in response to the gospel.

The Authority of Jesus

Matthew portrays Jesus as a king with authority. This authority is seen and recognized by the Roman centurion (8:8-9), a scribe (8:19), the disciples (8:27), the demons (8:29), and the crowds (9:8). Later on in the narrative, Matthew shows how Jesus as the supreme authority came into conflict with those who represented lesser authorities. First, Jesus comes into sharp conflict with the political authorities (14:1-14). Then he meets the religious authorities (15:1-21). And finally, Matthew shows Jesus in conflict with the representatives of Jewish nationalism and racism (15:21-28). Jesus calls those to follow him whose loyalty will transcend that of all lesser loyalties of race or of nation, of religious tradition or of politics, for to Him is due the supreme allegiance. The will of God is far more important than any religious tradition or observance, and it alone has a prior claim upon one's entire being and life.

All four writers mention the entry of Jesus into Jerusalem, although they differ in the details with which they describe it. Matthew carefully describes the setting and narrates the event, always picturing Jesus as the Messiah-King who is the fulfillment of the Jewish hope and of Messianic prophecy.

It has been said that Mark's Gospel could well
be called "The Deeds of Jesus," for it is a story of
action, portraying Jesus as a doer more than as a
teacher. Certainly there is no attempt to write a
full biography of Jesus. Mark begins with Jesus as
an adult, with no mention of Bethlehem, the Wise
Men, the shepherds, the angels, Mary, or Joseph;
there is no genealogy; nothing is said of Jesus as a
boy. This is a dramatic and direct story, in which
the author presents Jesus as the Son of God, the expected Messiah. Even John the Baptist gets very
little attention in Mark. The reference to John
seems to be more of an introduction to the ministry
of Jesus than anything else.

A Story of Action

There is no place to pause for rest in the account
by Mark. He has a story to tell, and he tells it rap-
idly and dramatically. We have to hasten to keep
up with him.

More than forty times the word "straightway" is
used in this Gospel, or as it is usually translated in
the Revised Standard Version, "immediately." A
few examples of this rapid action in Mark are these
selections: After the baptism of Jesus, "the Spirit
immediately drove him out into the wilderness"
(1:12). Jesus called Andrew and Simon, "and immediately they left their nets and followed him"
(1:18). Jesus saw James and John, "and immediately he called them" (1:20). They went into Capernaum, "and immediately on the sabbath he entered
the synagogue and taught" (1:21). After Jesus had

touched the daughter of Jairus, "immediately the girl got up and walked" (5:42). When the five thousand had been fed, "immediately he made his disciples get into the boat and go before him to the other side" (6:45)

Matthew seemed to try to convince the Jews that Jesus was the Messiah by amassing evidence, showing the fulfillment of prophecy, and drawing heavily upon the Old Testament. There is none of that in Mark. He seems to have the idea that if he can simply show people how Jesus really lived and what he did, they will surely believe on him as the Son of God.

There is some evidence that this Gospel was written to the Gentile world rather than to the Jews. Here are some of the reasons usually given for that statement:

1. Mark has no genealogy, as do Matthew and Luke.

2. There are very few quotations from the Old Testament, whereas Matthew deliberately drew heavily upon the Old Testament.

3. Mark does not emphasize any fulfillment of prophecy; the action of Jesus stands by itself, not in relation to prophecy.

4. When certain Jewish names or customs or terms are used, the author gives a brief explanation of them, as in 1:44; 7:3-4, 11; 12:18; 15:22. If we know to whom the book is addressed, it helps us to understand why certain things are included or left out, why particular emphases are made, and why one book differs from another.

Mark also presents Jesus as one who is engaged in a terrific struggle with the forces of evil from the time of the temptation in the wilderness on through the narrative. He is in conflict with the powers of evil as he casts out the unclean spirits. When the people saw these acts of authority they were filled with awe and amazement, as Mark tells us over and over again. They had the same reaction to the skill he demonstrated in meeting the opposition of the religious leaders.

THE GOSPEL OF LUKE

There is no doubt about the purpose which inspired Luke to write his Gospel. It is stated explicitly in the opening paragraph (1:1-4). While he is not trying to give a complete biography, Luke does write an orderly and historical account of the life of Jesus. Assurance comes to the reader as he sees that Luke not only says he intends to give an accurate and historical account, but does page by page unfold his narrative accurately and in an orderly manner.

This story of the life of Jesus is different from the other Gospels in many ways. It seems to be written to the Gentile world, and portrays Jesus as the Christ who came first to the Jews, then to the entire world. Luke gives us a Christ whose appeal and whose concern for people is universal. When it was first read by the early Christians, it must have inspired them greatly, for it shows that in their allegiance to Jesus Christ they have become a part of a great world movement, a movement of triumph and victory. It is a pageant which portrays the victorious sweep of the early Christian movement, starting at Bethlehem and going to Jerusalem, then in the Acts of the Apostles going on to Rome itself. Those who read the book in the early days must have been caught up with the fact that God was doing a tremendous work with them and through them and for them. That same note is needed today, when people again must catch the view of Christianity as a universal movement in the plan of God, with ultimate victory assured those who follow faithfully.

Where Matthew gave us the story of the visit of the Wise Men, Luke tells us of the visit of the shepherds to the manger and omits any reference to the Wise Men. Again let us remind ourselves that each writer surely knew much, much more of the life and teachings of Jesus than he narrates; he simply selected those events and happenings which he wanted to put into his story. The omission of other events does not mean they did not occur, but simply that the writer was not especially interested in them at the particular moment of writing and for his own particular purpose. The contrast in the way Matthew and Luke begin the public ministry of Jesus is further evidence of the selectivity of each writer.

Luke presents Jesus as having gone out of his way to appeal to the Jews, but shows also how the Jewish leaders persisted in their rejection of Jesus as their Messiah-King. In the Gospel of Luke there is a much more favorable attitude toward Jesus shown by the Gentiles than by the Jewish leaders.

Luke emphasizes what we might call the winsomeness of Jesus. Jesus is portrayed as the expression of the love of God, a personality tenderly appealing to the outcasts and the downtrodden, full of mercy and compassion, always understanding and helpful.

Jesus Belongs to the World

Luke is aware of events of contemporary history, and writes his narrative in relation to the whole world in which Jesus lived. To him Jesus belongs to the world and cannot be confined to the nationalistic and narrow ideas of the Jews. Jesus is the Son of God, the Son of a gracious and merciful God, who has come into the world to bring healing to all the nations. And Luke tells that story with deep feeling. He is excited and moved by all that has happened. He cannot write in a matter-of-fact way because his story is so thrilling, so wonderful, so breath-taking. Luke tells how God has visited his people through his Son Jesus Christ. Such a story can never be told in dreary monotony if one feels it half as keenly as Luke felt it.

The Appeal to the Disadvantaged

It is in Luke that we see the attitude of Jesus toward the unfortunate, the poor, the women, and the children. In the day in which Jesus lived, women did not have the status they have in America today. They were little more than the property of men; Jesus gave them a new sense of worth and of dignity, as the Gospel of Luke shows. Elizabeth, the mother of John the Baptist, and Mary, the mother of Jesus, hold the spotlight in the early part of this book. When the baby Jesus was taken by his parents to the Temple, not only is Simeon mentioned, but Luke tells also about the prophetess, Anna. Jesus heals Peter's mother-in-law, the woman who pushed through the crowd to touch the fringe of his garment, and the daughter of Jairus. Among the other women whom Luke mentions are the widow who placed her offering in the treasury at the Temple, Mary Magdalene, Joanna, and Mary the mother of James.

Luke stresses the appeal which Jesus had for the poor. He has selected those teachings of Jesus which show the right and the wrong use of wealth. In such stories as the Parable of the Prodigal Son and the Parable of the Rich Man and Lazarus, Luke not only shows the winsome Jesus appealing to the poor, but even implies that wealth and riches might be a hindrance to effective discipleship. It takes all of these various stories to give us the true picture of Jesus.

Jesus and Prayer

The Gospel of Luke emphasizes the prayer life of Jesus. This is important, for we cannot understand the life of Jesus unless we see him in prayer. These glimpses into the hours of prayer show one who counted communion with the Father the most important part of his life. Prayer, to Jesus, was not a ritual to be performed, but the very life line to the Father; it was as natural to Jesus as flying is to a bird. Luke gives us two parables about prayer in addition to the record of the six occasions on which Jesus prayed during his ministry. These six occasions, of course, are only illustrations of the place Jesus gave to prayer.

The fact that Luke was a physician may account for his unusual interest in the healings performed in the ministry of Jesus. It is Luke who shows us the Jesus who could not stand to see men hungry, who wanted the poor to be clothed, who could not pass by the lame or the blind without touching them with his healing hand.

We are indebted to Luke for a fuller narrative of the Perean ministry than the other Gospels give, although it is sometimes difficult to say exactly which events and which teachings should be assigned to this period.

During the ministry in Perea, it is probably that Jesus and his disciples visited many places: "After this the Lord appointed seventy others, and sent them on ahead of him, two by two, into every town and place where he himself was about to come" (10:1).

In this period, also, we have a chance to see Jesus as he meets little children and their mothers. Three writers tell about this event (Mark 10:13-16; Matt. 19:13-15; Luke 18:15-17) which would indicate that it was unusual. The fact that the mothers felt free to bring their children to Jesus and the readiness with which the children accepted Jesus might suggest that Jesus had been in this vicinity for some time. He and the disciples had different views regarding children. The disciples evidently felt that Jesus had work to do which was much more important than chatting with children, but Jesus rebuked them and insisted that the children should have a place in his friendship and his ministry. The heart of Jesus is always open to the tears or the smiles of a child.

The story about the rich young ruler indicates the insight which Jesus had into the hearts of men. He could see deep down beneath the surface to the real needs of men. We can approach Christ today with full assurance that our needs are known better to him than they are to ourselves.

Jesus and the Jewish Leaders

In this period of his ministry Jesus teaches very clearly against certain attitudes which prevailed among the Jewish leaders. First, he struck out against the nationalistic tendencies of the Jews. They felt superior because they were Jews, and must have smarted under this emphasis of Jesus (10:25-37; 17:11-19). He taught against the misuse of wealth (12:13-21; 16), which had made oppressors and overlords out of the religious leaders. He disapproved the class distinctions being made (18:10). And he cried out against the attitude which placed temporal things first (17:33). Jesus made it clear in this ministry that anything which diverts one's supreme loyalty from God is either wrong or is receiving the wrong emphasis.

The three stories in the fifteenth chapter, the Lost Sheep, the Lost Coin, and the Lost Son are rich parables found only in Luke. We should be the poorer without them. They open to us the true attitude of God toward those whose lives are outside his will and purpose. They show the attitude of Jesus toward those who have missed the way or who have the wrong center of life.

It may be helpful to call brief attention to some ways in which Luke differs from the other Gospel writers in the account of the last days in Jerusalem, the arrest, trial, and crucifixion. Luke makes no mention of the trial before Caiaphas and Annas, but he does tell of the trial before Pilate. Only Luke mentions the trial before Herod. Luke is careful to tell us that two Roman officials had pronounced Jesus innocent of the charges against him (23:13-16). Luke records that while Jesus was bearing the cross through the streets of Jerusalem,

some women wept and cried out in sympathy for
him, but that Jesus did not accept their sympathy;
he knew that the days of trouble which lay ahead
for them would make many a woman sorry that she
had ever borne children (23:27-31).

Matthew, Mark, and John all record simply that
two others were crucified with Jesus. Luke, however, tells us that one of the criminals repented in his
last hour, and that Jesus, in true self-forgetfulness,
graciously received the repentance and freely gave
forgiveness. Such a snapshot as this incident re-
veals helps us to get a good picture of Jesus, as he
forgot his own pain and trouble to minister to a
dying thief who had turned to him for help.

THE GOSPEL OF JOHN

When we turn to the Gospel of John for an account of the life of Jesus, we seem to move into a
situation quite different from the accounts of the
Synoptic writers, Matthew, Mark, and Luke. The
style is different, the language is different, the purpose is different. Our concern at this point is not
with any critical problem, but with the picture of
Jesus and the teachings of Jesus which are given in
this Gospel.

We have seen that Matthew wrote to the Jews,
and that he used prophecy and the Old Testament
as among the chief means of proving to them that
Jesus was their expected king, the Messiah; we
have seen that Mark portrayed Jesus as a divine
worker of miracles, who would win men's allegiance if only they could see him in his true light.
In Luke we have found a message addressed more
to the Gentile world, portraying Jesus Christ as a

universal Savior. John's Gospel was written much later, and undoubtedly on the assumption that these other three Gospels were rather familiar to most people. Therefore this writer gives not only a record of the life and deeds of Jesus, but, more than that, he gives an interpretation; for that reason John has been called the "spiritual" Gospel. The author writes with conviction and an explicit purpose (20:31) which is to convince men that Jesus is the Christ and to win their undying loyalty to him.

The Divinity of Jesus Portrayed

All four writers portray a Person who is the highest we can imagine, and who goes far beyond the highest of any human standard. But whereas Matthew, Mark, and Luke relate those incidents which seem to emphasize the humanity of Jesus, John selects those incidents which bring out his divinity. He does not begin with a genealogy or any account of the birth of Jesus; there is no manger scene and no wondrous night at Bethlehem; there are no hushed and awe-filled shepherds, no majestic Wise Men following a star through nameless nights to a babe worthy of their adoration: John dips his pen deeper than history, back in the very beginning, and there he finds this Son of God.

Though he omits many events which are included by the other writers, we must not think that John is denying them; he is only selecting the incidents which fit in with the picture of the Christ he wants us to see.

The account of the baptism of Jesus is given as a sign to John the Baptist; there is no reference to the wilderness experience of temptation, no prayer for a renewal of his own strength, no cry for help on the cross.

John and the Synoptic Writers

We might think from the Synoptic writings that the ministry of Jesus began after John the Baptist had been imprisoned; but in the Gospel of John there seems to be an overlapping of the public ministries of Jesus and John the Baptist (3:22-24). The ministry of Jesus as recorded by John occurred mostly in Judea and Jerusalem, with only brief trips into Galilee; in the other Gospels most of the incidents are taken from the Galilean ministry, and Jesus journeys to Jerusalem only for the last events leading up to his crucifixion. There is also a difference in the length of the ministry of Jesus. In John the ministry lasted about three years, whereas the other writers give the impression that it was not more than one year in length. It will be helpful to remind ourselves again, at this point, that none of these writers is giving a biography of Jesus or a story of the life of Jesus intended to be accurate chronologically; that was not in their thinking or intention. Hence we can expect many differences in these accounts because of the purposes of the writings themselves.

Let us look briefly, now, at some of the more outstanding and characteristic features of the Gospel of John as he portrays Jesus to us.

The "Word" Was God

The use of the untranslatable word *Logos* in John may be confusing to us today, but it was perfectly clear to the Greek mind for which John

wrote. The Greek philosophers of John's day spoke
of a logos which was an agency of God in creation
and revelation, but their logos was impersonal and
abstract. John picks up their own terminology and
says, in effect, "While you have been searching for
the logos, an impersonal intermediary between
God and man, we have found the true logos, the
creator of the universe, the true revelation of God.
Our logos is not abstract and impersonal. He was
with God and was God, and he 'became flesh and
dwelt among us . . . ; we have beheld his glory.' "
To John, then, Jesus is the true Logos, the Son of
God who became flesh, the creator and sustainer of
all things and of life itself. He does not use the
word logos again after this first chapter, but all
through the book are his references to light, life,
and truth as found in Jesus.

Also in John's day there were some who tried to
make a case for Jesus as a spiritual being without
human form. John, it is said, makes it clear that
Jesus was both human and divine.

With all four Gospels together, then, we have a
glorious picture of One who is God, who is the creator of the universe, the author of life itself, but
who is both human and divine. As the Son of God
he is eternal; as the Jesus of history he was born in
the little town of Bethlehem. As the Jesus of history he was crucified on the cross of Calvary; as the
eternal Son of God he lives today and forevermore.

The Gospel of John contains only seven stories of
the miracles of Jesus, while Mark gives us thirty-
eight. In John there are no parables given; contrast
this with just one chapter of Luke, the fifteenth,
where the sublime parables of the Lost Sheep, the
Lost Coin, and the Lost Boy are given. John has
carefully selected the seven miracles he relates, and

each one is used as a parable, or for a teaching purpose.

The Miracles Also Teach

John does not stop with telling how and when and where Jesus healed a blind man. He uses that bit of historic fact as the illustration of his teaching that Jesus is the "light of the world." This symbolism is found in the use of the other miracles also. The details of the raising of Lazarus are carefully recounted so that we know this is a real miracle, not simply a fanciful tale, but the whole incident is used as an illustration or a symbol of Jesus' teaching that he is "the resurrection and the life." Feeding of the five thousand is a miracle beyond question, carefully told so that we can easily reconstruct the scene in our own minds; John uses the story, though, for a greater purpose. It becomes the vehicle for the teaching of Jesus: "My Father gives you the true bread from heaven. For the bread of God is that which comes down from heaven, and gives life to the world. . . . I am the bread of life; he who comes to me shall not hunger, and he who believes in me shall never thirst" (6:32-33, 35).

The Gospel of John is pre-eminently the Gospel of love—the love of God. It is from John's record of the conversation between Jesus and Nicodemus that we get the one scripture which is probably better known to more people than any other in the entire Bible (3:16), and it is a scripture of the love of God. When Lazarus was near death John records that "the sisters sent to him, saying, 'Lord, he whom you love is ill'" (11:3). Later, when Jesus was so "deeply moved in spirit and troubled" that he wept, the Jews who stood by said, "See how he loved him!" (11:36). And when we read such an account as that given by John (5:2-9) of the healing of the sick man at the pool of Bethzatha, *we* feel like saying, "Behold what manner of love this Jesus has!"

John will not let Jesus be confined to any narrow nationalism. To John this Son of God belongs to all mankind, to the whole world. His vocabulary stresses the universal appeal of Jesus. He stresses the experiences common to all men everywhere, such as hunger, thirst, love, and the desire for life after death. We see Jesus Christ, then, the fulfillment of Old Testament prophecy, the Messiah of the Jews, and also the Savior and Lord of every man and woman of any race and nation who will confess Him and accept him by faith.

Topics for Further Thought

1. A harmony of the Gospels will be very helpful to you as you study this chapter. Compare, first of all, the way the Gospels begin.

2. Compare Matthew 13 with Mark 4. Why is there repetition of material in the Gospels?

3. List and compare the reasons each writer had for producing his Gospel.

4. Compare the audiences to whom the various Gospels are written.

5. Make a list of some of those things that are found in the Synoptic Gospels that are not found in the Gospel of John.

6. Would it make any difference in your church, in your town, in your community, if the principles laid down in Luke 14:7-14 were followed every day?

7. How much of the material in Luke, chapters 9 to 19, can be found in Mark? Why?

8. Look up the meaning of the word "disciple." Can you give in a sentence the standard which Jesus set for his disciples?

CHAPTER V

WHAT DID JESUS TEACH?

The first thing that ought to be said in this chapter is that Jesus did not teach facts or principles; he taught people! There is a vast difference between teaching persons and teaching facts. Jesus apparently did not have an organized body of knowledge which he wanted to impart to his followers. Rather he observed the needs of people and tried to show them how to live as God wanted them to live. He tried to show them how they should treat each other, how they should regard property, what their relations with the government should be, how they should think of God—because these and other similar questions represented areas of need.

It is difficult to separate what Jesus taught from the commonly accepted body of Christian teaching. Christian teaching involves the entire New Testament, whereas in this study we are primarily concerned with what Jesus taught. This is not a systematic study of Christian doctrine, in other words,

but a survey of the accounts of Jesus' teachings as
they are recorded in the four Gospels.

What Jesus Taught About the Kingdom

Mark says that the first sermon Jesus preached
was a sermon about the kingdom of God, "The
time is fulfilled, and the kingdom of God is at
hand" (1:15). Throughout the entire ministry of
Jesus the one dominant note that we hear is the
kingdom of God. It was a watchword or slogan
with Jesus, but it was much more than that. There
are not many parables which do not begin with the
words, "The kingdom of God is like . . ." or "The
kingdom of heaven is like . . ."

To the Jews there was nothing new about this
phrase. The phrase itself had a familiar ring from
the preaching of the prophets of Israel. The coming
of the kingdom of God was more prominent in the
thinking of the Jews than any other one idea. They
hoped for it, they prayed for it, they lived for the
day when the kingdom of God would come. The
idea, the phrase itself was not new; it was the
meaning Jesus gave it, the way he used the term,
that made it different with Jesus.

As we have already seen, the only hope the Jews
had of release from Roman domination was that
God would intervene and usher in the Kingdom. In
the day of Jesus that hope was white-hot. At the
same time, the content of the phrase had changed
from the meaning the Old Testament prophets had
given it. With the Jews in the time of Jesus the
idea of the kingdom of God was shot through with
secular and materialistic hopes. The Kingdom
would bring release from Roman domination; the

Jews would be exalted as rulers; prosperity would be their lot.

What Is the Kingdom of God?

Jesus took this phrase, then, and packed it full of new and higher meaning.

In the first place, the kingdom of God, according to Jesus, is a spiritual kingdom. It is not a political kingdom. It is the reign of God in the hearts of men. It promises no earthly wealth or power or possessions. Jesus forever rejected that concept when he rejected the suggestion of the Tempter in the wilderness to make bread out of stones. Jesus makes no promise that his followers will have physical comforts; in fact, the very opposite is true. There is nothing secular nor materialistic about Jesus' concept of the Kingdom. "The kingdom of God is not coming with signs to be observed; nor will they say, 'Lo, here it is!' 'There!' for behold, the kingdom of God is in the midst of you" (Luke 17:20-21).

This kingdom of God is universal. The Jews were intensely nationalistic in their outlook. They wanted a kingdom for themselves with everyone else beneath them. Jesus said the kingdom of God is in the hearts of men, and one's nationality has nothing to do with his membership in the Kingdom. Jesus was crucified because he refused to set up a kingdom such as the Jewish leaders wanted. When he lifted the kingdom of God above Jewish nationalism, he also lifted up the cross for himself.

Fellowship and Brotherhood

The kingdom of God is God's rule over that fellowship which is his family. There is no room here for unrelated individuals. The individual comes into his highest worth and dignity under the teaching of Jesus; the Kingdom is made up of all these worthful individuals together. We very easily get into theological tangles over the relation of the Kingdom and the church. In the concept of the Kingdom which Jesus used there is a social or group fellowship of people who have a common allegiance and a common Lord. It was not the Jews as such who would enter the Kingdom, but whoever would do the will of God. "And looking around on those who sat about him, he said, 'Here are my mother and my brothers! Whoever does the will of God is my brother, and sister, and mother'" (Mark 3:34-35).

The standards of the Kingdom are set forth in the Sermon on the Mount, recorded most fully in Matthew (5—7) and in passages in Luke. The Beatitudes may be thought of as a brief summary of those qualities of personality and character found in those who make up the kingdom of God.

The kingdom of God is not a future hope, a dream, a "far-off divine event," but a present reality. It began in a small way and grows. It began in the hearts of some of those people who heard Jesus talk about it and who then and there surrendered their lives to his control. "And he said, 'With what can we compare the kingdom of God, or what parable shall we use for it? It is like a grain of mustard seed, which, when sown upon the ground, is the smallest of all the seeds on earth; yet when it is sown it grows up and becomes the greatest of all shrubs, and puts forth large branches, so that the birds of the air can make nests in its shade'" (Mark 4:30-32). The Kingdom is in a struggle against sin, ignorance, greed, cruelty, selfishness and all evil, but the ultimate victory belongs to God. In that sense the Kingdom is the reign of God now in the hearts of men and the assurance that God shall reign in the hearts of men.

What Jesus Taught About God

The Father was very real to Jesus. Jesus never questions or attempts to prove the existence of God, for the reality of the relationship between the Son and the Father was greater than any other proof could be. Jesus felt at home in a world made by the heavenly Father for his children and saw in all of it the creative handiwork of God. The lilies of the field are clothed by God; the birds that neither sow nor reap nor gather into barns are cared for by God.

Nothing can escape the attention of God because it is too small or too insignificant. God is like a shepherd who knows and cares when just one sheep is outside the fold. God is like a woman who thoroughly sweeps the house to find one coin she has lost. When a little sparrow falls to the ground, we neither know nor care; God both knows and cares. And Jesus taught that God does this directly, without any of the intermediaries characteristic of the religions of the world. All things are possible with God; therefore all things are possible to the man who trusts completely in God.

God Is Good

God alone is good. Jesus taught us that, and he taught that the goodness of God is ever creative and active. God's goodness and concern for each person made him so real and so near that Jesus called him "Father." God is king, but God is pre-eminently Father. He is concerned for each individual person in the world; not a sparrow can fall without his notice, and *any* person is worth more than *many* sparrows! With an idea like that, one can never think of people as a means to an end. People are ends in themselves. Privileged groups dare not exploit the less fortunate or the oppressed because that violates the essential goodness of God as expressed in his care for persons.

God Is Loving and Forgiving

God is like that father who ran out to meet his wayward but penitent son, and who met the prodigal sinner with a prodigality of love and mercy. Jesus taught that the heart of God was moved to forgiveness by the sincere prayer of a publican who cried, "God be merciful to me a sinner." To win all men to dedication of heart and life is the desire of God. "Even so, I tell you, there will be more joy in heaven over one sinner who repents than over ninety-nine righteous persons who need no repentance" (Luke 15:7).

The essential good will of God is not limited, but flows out freely to all men everywhere, even to those who have refused that love and care. "But I say to you, Love your enemies and pray for those who persecute you, so that you may be sons of your Father who is in heaven; for he makes his sun rise on the evil and on the good, and sends rain on the just and on the unjust" (Matt. 5:44-45). Such a belief in God undergirds all of life with buoyant faith and strong confidence. Nothing can really harm a person who trusts in a God like that. Pain may come, of course, and temporal reverses, but in the long run victory is assured, and the pure in heart shall see their God.

God Is Righteous and Holy

There is another aspect to Jesus' teaching about God. Jesus stood right alongside the prophets of Israel in his teaching that punishment is certain and sure for the man who willfully sets his will against that of God, who spurns God's offer of love and forgiveness. Jesus clearly set before men the two ways, one to life and the other to death. Jesus sought no truce with evil because evil is forever opposed to God.

Jesus taught us that more than anything else God seeks the loving allegiance of men and women—seeks that more than any amount of formal worship or obedience to law. "Jesus answered, 'The first is, "Hear, O Israel: The Lord our God, the Lord is one; and you shall love the Lord your God with all your heart, and with all your soul, and with all your mind, and with all your strength"'" (Mark 12:29-30).

To Jesus God was a Father with whom conversation, through prayer, was the most natural thing in the world. Prayer was not a ritual nor a religious performance, because God was personal and real to Jesus. Prayer was ritualistic and self-centered to many of the Pharisees simply because they had no intimate personal relationship with God.

Jesus taught that at the heart of this universe is a God of love, whose desire is to bring all mankind into fellowship and likeness with himself, and that the richest blessings of God await those who accept this love, while the consequences of persistent rejection are inexorable and sure.

WHAT JESUS TAUGHT ABOUT RIGHTEOUSNESS

Few people have ever been more concerned with righteousness than were the Jews of Jesus' day, and few who have been that concerned have ever missed it so completely. Their concept of righteousness was in careful, punctilious, detailed observance of the Law, so we shall not discuss it fully here. But the only kind of righteousness those Jewish leaders knew was in outward conformity and obedience to the ceremonial law.

Jesus expected more than that from his followers. "For I tell you, unless your righteousness exceeds that of the scribes and Pharisees, you will never enter the kingdom of heaven" (Matt. 5:20). Then Jesus proceeded to show how it must exceed, to show what he meant by righteous living.

Righteous living, Jesus taught, begins in the heart. It springs from inner attitudes which are of more importance to God than the outward actions. "You have heard that it was said, 'You shall not commit adultery.' But I say that every one who looks at a woman lustfully has already committed adultery with her in his heart" (Matt. 5:27-28). The first measure of any action, then, is the motive behind it, what prompted it, the attitude underlying it. True righteousness begins in a man's heart.

True righteousness allows for no insincerity or double-mindedness. To Jesus there was always one standard by which he judged everything: Is this the will of God for me? No personal convenience, no selfish whim or fancy, no thought of the effect on his own comfort, but only whether it was pleasing to the Father. The one dominant motive that characterized his life is right here.

The righteousness that Jesus taught is also expressed in the way we treat other people, the way we order our lives day by day. There is no isolation of religion from the everyday affairs of a man's life. The attitudes he holds in his heart will find some expression in the way he lives. "Not every one who says to me, 'Lord, Lord,' shall enter the kingdom of heaven, but he who does the will of my Father who is in heaven" (Matt. 7:21). Just as a tree can be identified by the fruit it bears, so a follower of Jesus will be known by the life he lives.

With Jesus there was no separation of life into compartments, no division of the religious and the secular. Life is one. A person is a unity, and the righteousness of God must claim the whole person. It is not only how a man acts on the day of worship that is important, but how he acts every day of every week. A man may guard his conversation carefully, but some chance word may give away his true nature. The righteousness Jesus taught is so complete and so thoroughgoing that it involves a completely new person, and under it a man is not ever afraid to stand the judgment of an idle word or a chance action.

The goodness of Jesus is much more than that which can be attained by human effort. It is more than ethical conduct. There is a certain "plus" which can be explained only by supernatural grace. It is that "plus" which ought to differentiate a Christian from another person who is morally good. Jesus came not to make men simply "good" but to open the door for them to "become sons of God."

Goodness with Jesus is always positive. Righteousness finds ways to serve. An inner urge moves the followers of Jesus to initiate enterprises of helpfulness. The Levite and the priest may not have been guilty of breaking the law, but they fell short of the righteousness of God. The rich man at whose gate lay Lazarus is not berated for anything except that his righteousness was not strong enough or deep enough to stir him to benevolent action. The unprofitable servant who was cast into outer darkness was condemned only for hiding his talent in the earth; he did nothing to improve that which his master had entrusted to his care. There is a certain "plus" in the life of Jesus that explains the kind of righteousness he taught, which must be found in our lives today also. It was not enough to refrain from strife; one should be a positive peacemaker. It was not enough to bear an insult without retaliation; one should turn the other cheek. It was not enough to do what one was compelled to do; he should go the second mile of willing and glad service. These ideas were not at all popular in the day when they were first expressed, nor are they popular today. They do not guarantee anything but the approval of God and the joy of righteous living. They led Jesus to a cross. It is not likely that this kind of righteousness will lead any of us today into comfortable or luxurious living. This kind of righteousness reaches into every little corner of everyday living; it is basic to the kingdom of God.

It is evident, then, that we cannot reduce righteous living to certain deeds or words or actions. It involves the whole person all the time. That person must be constantly growing, reaching, achieving the higher and the better.

WHAT JESUS TAUGHT ABOUT SERVICE

"He who is the least among you all is the one who is great" (Luke 9:48). These words of Jesus must have sounded strange to a people who thought of greatness in connection with power and authority. They are strange words for our day, too. There must have been "social climbers" in the world Jesus knew just as there are today. The disciples themselves were not immune to this temptation. "And an argument arose among them as to which of them was the greatest" (Luke 9:46). Through the centuries there have been people—otherwise good folk—who have given their whole lives to climbing to the top in one field or another, even in the church. Position, power, and prestige have lured them onward, but not always upward.

In the face of all that, here is Jesus saying that the truly great person is he who is the servant of all. It is a law of life, but one we easily overlook. In the long run, it is not "pull" or "knowing the right person" that makes one great. Those may be factors in getting a certain job or position. But one writes his name on the hearts of his fellow men with indelible ink just in the measure to which he serves. "For whoever would save his life will lose it; and whoever loses his life for my sake and the gospel's will save it" (Mark 8:35).

WHAT JESUS TAUGHT ABOUT POSSESSIONS

One does not have to be either poor or rich to be struck with the teachings of Jesus about possessions. His message here is for all of us—the poor, the wealthy, the middle class.

Jesus did not condemn the possession of wealth as such. He did not condemn the rich young ruler (Luke 18:18-25), but he did use the occasion to point out the temptation to misuse money. In the Parable of the Talents, the only person condemned was the man who had the least—only one talent of money—and he was called a "wicked servant." It is the way possessions are used that determines the judgment passed upon their owner.

Jesus did condemn the use of possessions as a means of exploiting the poor. He did teach against setting one's heart upon any material possessions (Matt. 6:19-21). He taught against *trust* in riches. The rich farmer who had to build new barns to take care of his crops was foolish for trusting in his wealth. He worked feverishly to amass enough wealth to be financially secure, only to find that it was of no help at all in facing the biggest problem of his life. By contrast, in the Sermon on the Mount, Jesus exalts that kind of trust in the heavenly Father which really believes God will take care of the material needs of the man who places the kingdom of God first.

Jesus himself came from a family that knew the pinch of want. It is probable that he toiled at hard work himself for some years to help support his widowed mother and the younger children of the family. He knew the peasant life, the drudgery of working day after day trying to "make both ends meet." He knew also the fat money bags of the Temple rulers. He knew the greed and the avarice that had swept over many of the Jewish leaders like an epidemic or a tidal wave.

Jesus taught, without any doubt, that God must rule the entire person and all he has. The kingdom of God can brook no rival for a man's loyalty and allegiance. Whenever the race for money gets fast, whenever anyone gets his eyes fixed on possessions so that they loom larger in his plans that does the will of God, then he has broken a fundamental law of life: no one can serve two masters. This tendency to give first place to money did not die, unfortunately, with the first century; it is still with us. Jesus taught, also, that men are worth more than money, and that in the kingdom of God it is not tolerable to sacrifice the claims of a person for anything material. And Jesus taught—how clearly!— against the sin of covetousness. To use one's possessions as a means of service to others, to place first the needs of human beings, to weigh every action in the scale of the will of God—these are principles Jesus gave us that still hold good today. There is room for only one *first* in the kingdom of God.

WHAT JESUS TAUGHT ABOUT LOVE

Words often change their meanings. Many times, also, a word loses some of its strength in the process of being translated from one language into another. Both of these facts apply to the word love as used by Jesus. The usual use of the word today carries the connotation of affection, whereas that is not very prominent in the term Jesus used. What Jesus meant by love is sometimes called "intelligent good will."

When Jesus says we are to love our enemies, can anyone say he meant to *feel* toward one's enemies the way one *feels* toward the members of his own family—wife, husband, children, parents? No, the love of God is greater, higher, stronger than that kind of love. The love of God is redemptive love. The love of God, as revealed by Jesus, frankly recognizes the depth to which any human being may go, such as the thief on the cross; but it gives itself redemptively to help that person become what God intended he should be. There is no love of God without giving; God so loved that he *gave*. God gave himself in the person of Jesus Christ his Son.

We are not called upon to *generate* the kind of love Jesus had for Judas, or Peter, or the dying thief. Rather we are asked to be the channels through which the love of God can flow to those who need it. In that way one can and must love his enemies. In that way one who loves his enemies will do good to those who use him despitefully. The love Jesus talked about was divine love, and must come to us from God, then out through our lives to a needy world of men and women.

The love we are asked to have for God—to love God with the whole heart and soul and mind—is an attitude of trust and faith, of loyalty and devotion. With such love one cannot place anything else first, anything which comes between one and God; to claim a lesser loyalty breaks that love and cannot be tolerated.

God is still at work in his world, working redemptively for mankind. We become workers together with him as we place ourselves at his disposal to be channels through whom that redeeming love can operate.

What Jesus Taught About Man

What Jesus taught about man affects all of us today. It was Jesus who gave man a sense of worth and his true dignity as a child of God. The soul of a man is beyond all price. "For what does it profit a man, to gain the whole world and forfeit his life? For what can a man give in return for his life?" (Mark 8:36-37).

People Are Important

Jesus did not think of men as pawns upon a big chessboard, to be moved by the caprice or fancy of any god or man. Each man must cast the decision for his own life and soul, and no other person can do it for him. "Whom say *ye* that I am?"

A man is more important than any religious rite or ritual. The Jews did not agree with Jesus. "And he said to them, 'The sabbath was made for man, not man for the sabbath; so the Son of man is lord even of the sabbath'" (Mark 2:27-28). It was important to Jesus to keep the law regarding the observance of the Sabbath, but not when that law stood in the way of ministering to a human need. Nothing could stand then.

The Compassion of Jesus

His attitude toward those who suffered brought such crowds to Jesus that some feared for his life. "And he told his disciples to have a boat ready for him because of the crowd, lest they should crush him; for he healed many, so that all who had diseases pressed upon him to touch him" (Mark 3:9-10). Wherever there were people, there was Jesus. Especially would he be found where there were people in need. He ate with sinners and tax collectors, which we have already seen was enough to incense the Jewish leaders against him. He talked with a Samaritan woman. That becomes more significant if we recall three things from the setting. First, this was a woman, and Jesus broke over the custom in giving her equal status with himself as a person. Second, she was a Samaritan, of a race despised by every good Jew. Finally, she was a great sinner, known to all her neighbors for her open sin. Jesus talked with her because she was a person in need; he met that need.

Jesus could not endure to see people suffer. He was "moved with compassion" to relieve their suffering. Five thousand people were just so many people to the disciples, but to Jesus they were five thousand separate individuals, every one of whom was hungry and ought to be fed. To the Jews, the raving madman among the tombs was just another man possessed with demons, but to Jesus he was a person in need, and Jesus set him free from his trouble. He stopped a funeral procession because there was a woman in deep need. A woman in the house of Simon the Pharisee was just a moral failure, an untouchable to Simon; to Jesus she was a person whose soul was hungry for the bread of life, and who responded with her whole soul to his understanding and forgiving love.

A Gospel of Redemption

Men and women are the hope of Jesus. He built his kingdom on the strength of that hope. He believed that if he surrounded himself with a few men who could see him day by day, share his hopes and dreams and aspirations, feel the burden of lost mankind as he felt it, see the possibilities in people that he saw, and catch the fire that burned in his own soul—these men in turn would go out in his name to turn the world upside down. They did! They did it because Jesus believed in them and God worked through them. As with Peter, so with all the rest, Jesus knew the worst, but believed for the best. To Jesus every man has a potential which should be realized. If the image of God upon his soul has been marred or blurred, then forgiving love will restore that soul. God does not wish one person to be lost to the fellowship of God. Jesus came to "seek and to save" all who are lost, to win them back to the Father, for "God is not willing that any should perish."

WHAT JESUS TAUGHT ABOUT SIN

Jesus did not discuss sin abstractly, but he did have something to say about it. He sometimes dealt with specific sins, but more often he traced sin back to the heart of man and pointed out the need of having a pure heart.

Central to the whole purpose of the coming of Jesus was this matter of sin and salvation from it. "Thou shalt call his name Jesus, for he shall save his people from their sins" (Matt. 1:21). "The Son of man is come to seek and to save that which was lost" (Luke 19:10). "For this is my blood of the covenant, which is poured out for many for the forgiveness of sins" (Matt. 26:28). "For God sent the Son into the world, not to condemn the world, but that the world might be saved through him" (John 3:17). The chief battle Jesus fought was with sin. The reason for his crucifixion was sin. The victory of the resurrection was a victory over sin.

Sin is the breaking of the law—but which law? The Jewish leaders said it was the Law of Moses and their traditions concerning it. Righteousness was a ceremonial matter, a strict keeping of the Law in outward performances. Jesus pointed out that the real law of God was an inner law in the heart of man, and that to break that law was worse than to break the Law of Moses.

Sin Is Alienation from God

In the story of the Lost Son (Luke 15) one is moved as much by the loneliness and anguish of the father as he is by the sufferings the prodigal boy brought upon himself. This surely gives some insight into what sin does to the heart of God. Jesus felt his own heart break as he saw his people turn away from the goodness and mercy of God. "O Jerusalem, Jerusalem, killing the prophets and stoning those who are sent to you! How often would I have gathered your children together as a hen gathers her brood under her wings, and you would not!" (Matt. 23:37).

The most terrible result of sin is not its moral or social distress, but alienation from God, thwarting God's purpose, breaking the heart of a loving Father who yearns for his children to have the very best. Jesus could not and did not treat sin lightly.

To him it was the most terrible thing in all the world. One look at the cross tells us what Jesus thought about sin.

Jesus recognized the power of sin to enslave a man, and it was to such enslaved people that Jesus came to "preach deliverance." Sin breaks the ties of fellowship. Sin sets man against man and class against class and nation against nation. Worse, it sets man against God. The utter isolation of a man who has rebelled against the loving Father is one of the results of sin.

A Gospel of Forgiveness

Jesus said, however, that he did not come to condemn, but to forgive. "Behold, the Lamb of God, who takes away the sin of the world!" (John 1:29). When a sinner met Jesus, his despair changed to radiant hope, because Jesus came to forgive sins. Zaccheus must have stood quite low in the estimation of his neighbors and fellow men, but when he climbed down out of the tree and walked beside Jesus down the road to his house, he began to feel that even he might have hope. The prodigal felt that he was no more worthy to be called the son of his father, scarcely worthy to be a servant; but the father, when he met his son trudging down the road toward home, rejoiced to forgive him, blot out the past, restore him to full sonship, and lavishly pour out the best for him.

Somewhere in every man there burns an ember which Jesus sees, and which loving sympathy and tender concern can fan into a flame of devotion. Jesus had a way of looking deep beneath the rough outside of a man and finding that burning ember of good desire. Jesus looked through the superficiality of men and saw their true nature. Then he refused to believe anything but their very best. He dared a man to live up to his highest. If a man could only see Jesus as Peter did, when after the denial Jesus looked at Peter, he could nevermore be content with life on the low flatlands of sin and selfishness; he would be haunted by that look of trust and expectancy. And he would surely fall down in humble penitence and devoted worship, to confess his own unworthiness and the glory of Jesus Christ.

Topics for Further Thought

1. Give as briefly as you can the main points in the teaching of Jesus regarding the kingdom of God. Contrast this with the popular ideas of his day in regard to the Kingdom.

2. Are the teachings of Jesus merely ideals toward which we ought to strive, or are they practicable, and can they be realized today?

3. Has anybody besides Jesus actually practiced the things he taught?

4. How does the idea of God in the Old Testament compare with the idea of God which Jesus gave?

5. List the various ways in which the disciples accepted Jesus and began to follow him. How many of them are identical?

6. Read Mark 8:34-38. Some have said that here is the key to the life of Jesus. Do you agree or not? Why?

7. If you made a list of the characteristics of little children, to whom Jesus said the kingdom belongs, how would it compare with the list of qualifications given in the Sermon on the Mount?

CHAPTER VI

TEACHING
THE LIFE OF JESUS

One cannot read the life of Jesus as we have it in the Gospels without realizing how much Jesus appealed to children. As we have seen, this is not presented equally by all four authors, yet we do know that Jesus loved boys and girls and that they responded wholeheartedly to him. Children will give that same response today when Jesus is presented in a way they can understand.

There is no artificiality in adapting the life of Jesus to the various age groups, for God himself has graded us. That is, God in his infinite wisdom has created us so that we are not born with mature abilities or capacities. At each age of life we are capable of a certain degree of understanding and comprehension, for so we are made by God himself. The wise and skillful teacher has learned the general characteristics and abilities and capacities of children in each age group and uses that knowledge to adapt his teaching to that group. And so it is in teaching the life of Jesus. The manner of presentation will necessarily vary with varying ages.

The suggestions in this chapter are intended to help the teacher make an effective adaptation.

LITTLE CHILDREN

This treatment cannot be exhaustive, but is intended only to be suggestive of ways to teach the life of Jesus.

For these children it is most important that the teacher be able to tell in story form certain parts of the life of Jesus. It is not so much our concern here that the children get facts and data about Jesus as it is that they hear stories which awaken a response of appreciation and interest. We are most concerned that these stories will cause them to like Jesus and to want to please him.

Abstract ideas have no place in the child's world. Much of the adult understanding of the life of Jesus will focus in certain abstract theological ideas, but those are entirely outside the range of the child's experience or understanding. For example, it would be quite useless to say that God is a Spirit, but a preschool child who has been rightly taught about Jesus can understand that God is like Jesus.

The hearts of these boys and girls are most responsive to love, perhaps more than at any other time of life; consequently, we should use those stories about Jesus that show his love and care and compassion for people. Some of these stories will be told over and over again, and it does not matter in the least whether they are told in chronological order or not.

What Does the Story Do to Children?

How we tell these stories is as important as what we tell. A boy just turning five years old flatly refused to say his prayers, either at the table or before going to bed at night. His mother was even more puzzled when, a few days later, her boy asked her to take down from the wall the picture of the boy Jesus which hung in his room. He not only wanted it taken down, but he ordered his mother to "burn it up and throw it away!" Later the mother got his reasons: Jesus had died a long time ago when some men killed him, and he did not want the picture of a dead man in his room. She traced the tragedy back to a Sunday-school class, when a well-meaning but certainly unskilled teacher had told her class about the crucifixion in very gruesome terms and did not even go on to tell the resurrection story. Children *should* be taught something about the crucifixion, but there is no justifiable reason for shattering the simple faith of a little child, when careful selection of storytelling material and method would preserve all the values of faith and trust.

The stories preschool children should hear are those that are within the range of their experience. A child can understand how Jesus would be helpful and kind to a blind man, though he cannot understand the more mature aspects of the ministry of Jesus. A child can understand a story of Jesus helping a sick boy, and will respond to such a story well told. In response to such a story even a three- or four-year-old child might say, "Billy is sick; maybe we can do something to help him." That story evokes a response because it is within the range of the child's experience, it is something he can understand, and it kindles his imagination as it appeals both to his mind and to his emotions.

For children of this age there is no value at all in trying to teach the life of Jesus as such. Rather it is important to carefully select those events from the life of Jesus which can be told in simple, appealing stories within the limits of the child's own experience. Several stories can be chosen and told, all of which may teach the same basic truths: Jesus cares for people; Jesus is kind; Jesus is helpful; Jesus liked to go to church, and so forth. "Tell me a story" is probably one of the most frequent things a child says to one whom he loves; "Now, tell me another" may be just as frequent. Jesus himself recognized this truth about the teaching-learning process even on the adult level when he couched his most profound teachings in simple, appealing stories, or parables.

PRIMARY CHILDREN

The primary child is in public school and is learning to read. It may be helpful to guide him in the selection of passages from the Gospels which he can read and easily comprehend. However, he also responds quickly to well-told stories. The experiences and interests of the primary child are expanding in many ways; he is gaining new friends, going to school, learning to read, learning self-expression in writing; he is away from home "on his own" for many hours every day. The selections from the Gospels may well be chosen to match this growing and expanding world in which the primary child lives.

He will respond with interest to a story based on the experiences of Jesus as a boy in school. These are not told explicitly in the Gospels, of course, but are implicit in any study of the life of Jesus. Stories based on Jesus' attitude toward his parents will have real value to these children.

They will respond eagerly to stories that assure them of God's loving care and protection and to those that awaken a desire to be helpful. That desire should always be given some channel of expression, for children learn by doing. One class of primary children studied some of the stories of the healing ministry of Jesus and coupled their study to class projects of service. Each child on one Sunday in the summer was asked to bring a flower from home; the children arranged all the flowers in a bouquet and took them to an elderly lady who was a shut-in living close to the church building. There they presented their flowers, sang, and said simple prayers for a woman whose week was happier because of the music and laughter of little children. And the children were learning thoughtful consideration of others as they acted out their version of a simple Gospel story.

Many of the events of the life of Jesus can be dramatized by these boys and girls. Usually it is better to have no one act the part of Jesus, but to have the teacher reverently read the words which would come from Him. Anyone who doubts needs only to watch the reaction of any primary child to a story from the life of Jesus as one of the better-type radio programs might present it. These children need stories into which they can project themselves, and to which they can respond with some action.

Juniors will be interested in Jesus as a man, a man of action and of power, a hero of the very highest order. Jesus as he is presented in the Gospel of Mark is pre-eminently a man of activity and decisive movement. This side of Jesus appeals to juniors. They should have those parts of the narrative of Jesus' life which move quickly both within any given episode and in geographic location. It is neither necessary nor helpful to "moralize" for juniors—or for anyone, for that matter. The stories of Jesus can stand on their own merit and will speak to the interest and spiritual need of the juniors without tacking on any extra moral application. The juniors will see the implications for their own lives which any episode from the life of Jesus may hold for them.

The might and power of Jesus never ceased to amaze the people of his own day. They will be equally interesting to juniors today. The stories of the power of Jesus over the wind and the sea, over sickness and death, the power to open blind eyes and to forgive sins are all graphic portrayals which should interest any junior.

Systematic Study of Life of Jesus

Prior to this age there has been little emphasis upon a systematic study of the life of Jesus. Now, however, the boys and girls should get acquainted with Jesus as a person, and should have a fairly clear idea of the sequence of events in his life. This calls for teaching them the main chronological divisions of his life. It calls also for some knowledge of

Palestinian geography so that at least the provinces and principal towns and cities can be identified.

Outline maps of Palestine will help fix rather definitely certain boundaries and locations and identifications.

Teach for Decisions

Juniors are making choices that will soon lead to the great choice of their lives, and it is important that they see a dramatic portrayal of the choices their great Hero made in the light of the Father's will. Here is a leader who can and will capture the imagination and loyalty of juniors if his life is rightly presented.

It is very important that in presenting Jesus as the ideal man, one also portrays him as Lord and Savior of all of life. Some of the juniors will be making their decision for Christ in these years. That decision should be so well grounded that these boys and girls can hold it against the world. An alert teacher will be watching for that moment when Christ has become so appealing and is calling so insistently that one or more of the boys or girls in the class are ready to say "Yes" to all of the claims of discipleship which he can understand. It is not enough to present the historical Jesus as a person, or that juniors know the interesting narratives of his life. He must be so presented that sometime every boy and girl who hears the story of his love will also hear him say, "Behold, I stand at the door and knock."

Some of the parables of Jesus are much better teaching material for this age group than are others. For example, although the Parable of the Sower (Mark 4:1-20) is carefully explained by

Jesus himself, juniors would more easily grasp the truth of the Parable of the Mustard Seed, which follows in the next chapter (5:30-32). The central idea of this latter parable can easily be illustrated by showing on a map or a globe the expansion of Christianity throughout the world. Or, to choose an example from Luke, the Parable of the Good Samaritan (Luke 10:30-37) is much more within the comprehension of juniors than is the Parable of the Importunate Friend (11:5-13;). It is not so much the vocabulary that is used as it is the *ideas* that are expressed to which we must give careful consideration. For if an idea itself is outside the range of comprehension, no amount of simplification of vocabulary or terminology is going to help much in bringing it inside.

Use Historical Backgrounds

Juniors should also be getting a clear knowledge and understanding of some of the customs of Palestine in the days of Jesus. Some of this will come in a study of the geography of Palestine. It is helpful for the boys and girls to know such elementary facts as the kind of houses people lived in, the kind of clothing they wore, the political situation of the Roman Empire, the general economic background of the time of Jesus, and the occupations common to that period. If Peter can be made to step out of the pages of the New Testament and really live for a child as a brawny, big, rough sailor, a poor peasant and simple fisherman, impetuous as the wind which filled the sails of his boat, an outspoken leader of men, yet with a heart responsive to the tender love of God—then Jesus will live for that child, too.

In teaching the life of Jesus to juniors, the so-called "life situation" approach should be used often. That is, no passage from the Gospels is chosen arbitrarily, read, and then examined to "see what this verse teaches." Rather a whole event is given, and as it is unfolded to the child it carries its implications for his own life and does its own teaching. How useless it would be to tell in a dramatic narrative the story of the Good Samaritan, and then follow by saying, "This parable teaches us to be kind to those in need." If the story is well read or well told, the boys and girls themselves will respond by suggesting ways they can express kindness and helpfulness to those who are in need.

JUNIOR HIGH YOUTH

It is well to remember that history is not merely a series of events, but rather the record of what people did in given situations and circumstances. So in teaching the life of Jesus to intermediates, or junior high young people, we are not trying to present just so many facts; we are trying to make a Person live for them. There is a basic and intense appeal which Christ has for these young people on which an alert teacher will capitalize.

The Idealism of Jesus

Among both boys and girls of this age, hero worship really comes into its own. What a wonderful opportunity to present the supreme Hero of all time! People all over our world recognize in Jesus the fulfillment of their hopes and highest aspirations. He is the Ideal, his the highest manhood. Jesus is not limited by race or nationality or color, but finds an answering response in youth of every nation and every race. A wise teacher, then, will seize the opportunity so to present Jesus that every boy and girl in the class will yield to Him the place of honor and of noble allegiance in his own heart. Junior high youth respond readily to the accounts of moral achievement in the life of Jesus, just as juniors want stories of action such as Mark records. Jesus should be presented as the one who achieved and realized the highest idealism the world has ever seen. We never need *say* that Jesus is a hero, but let his life carry its own appeal to junior high youth.

A good example of Jesus' idealism would be found in a study of the Sermon on the Mount. The average adult may say it is too idealistic, but its teachings will find a response in junior high youth if they can see that what Jesus taught he actually practiced in his own life.

Jesus Overcomes Temptation

Another teaching value is relevant to the many temptations which confront an intermediate boy or girl. A mere listing of some of their common temptations would be quite lengthy! And with those severe temptations comes the feeling of "aloneness"— the feeling that no one understands or cares. Without becoming soft or sentimental about it, a teacher can so present Jesus that the junior high youth will say to himself, "Jesus had some of the same hopes and dreams that I have; he had some of the fears and doubts that I have; he faced temptations similar to my own, or worse than those I face. Jesus was true to his ideals, and never once did he compromise them. If God is like Jesus, he does know and understand my problems, and will help to see me through."

Jesus Is Human and Divine

Some attention should be given in this age group to those facts in the Gospels which can be summoned to portray Jesus as a real man, an actual person, not simply a vague ideal long since removed from earth. For example, just what did occur when Jesus was lost in the Temple at Jerusalem at the age of twelve years? And what are the things that probably happened in the few years immediately following that episode? What kind of school did he attend, and what did he study there? What kind of work did he do? How and when did he get so well acquainted with nature and the out-of-doors?

One illustration of a simple presentation of Jesus as a person and as Lord of all could be used in a Sunday-morning worship for the junior high class or department. If the room can be darkened, throw on a screen the picture of Sallman's "Head of Christ," using a small slide projector. If the room cannot be darkened, a print—either framed or unframed—of this same picture could be hung at the front of the room against a simple velvet or monk's cloth drape. Perhaps a spotlight will be needed on the picture. From the New Testament let a member of the class read such a passage as Luke 9:7-20, which includes the great confession of Peter. A suitable hymn would be "Fairest Lord Jesus." A worship experience built on such a simple outline as that serves to focus all attention upon Jesus the Christ, and to call for the same sort of response which Peter gave.

These junior high young people will also give a hearty response to the ideals of service which are inherent in any study of the life of Jesus. Such events as those portrayed in the following passages will be most useful in portraying Him as one whose sympathy and care are extended to all people in need, whoever and wherever they may be: Luke 8:22-25, 26-39, 49-56; 9:37-43; 10:29-37; 13:10-17; John 5:1-18; 11:1-44.

SENIORS AND YOUNG PEOPLE

The first followers of Jesus were young people. The Christian movement was a youth movement. Jesus Christ has a strong appeal for young people today, which makes it easy to teach the life of Jesus to them.

Jesus as a Hero

The same idealism of Jesus which captured the imagination and loyalty of Peter, John, Andrew, and Thomas will win the allegiance of youth today. They still respond to the Master as the greatest hero of all time. Maybe it is because Jesus was such a young man when he ministered upon earth, or perhaps it is because these youthful days of confusion and change respond to the authority and dynamic leadership of Jesus; we know that here is an opportunity to win the loyalty of youth to Jesus the Christ.

There may be the temptation to present Jesus as an idealist. That he was, but he was also a realist. He saw men and women as they were; he also saw what they could become. He saw the ungodly conditions of the world about him; he also saw what the world could be. If we present Jesus only as an idealist, later in life the young people we teach will discover that there is sometimes a wide gap between the ideal and the actual. The Sermon on the Mount can be presented as an ideal, or it can be presented as that which can be attained through the power and the guidance of Christ.

Jesus was not simply an idealist whose dreams were impractical and otherwordly. He was the most practical person the world has ever known! His way of living has never been given a real chance in our world. When we do give it a chance we shall discover that the real secret of happy and abundant living was with Him all along.

It will be well to remember that Jesus, when he was crucified, was not just the victim of unsympathetic men. His death was not that of a martyr, willing to die for his ideals and dreams. If that were all, then Jesus becomes only another great hero of the world. We must present him to youth as more than that. He is the Christ, the Son of God. His death was voluntary; in some manner beyond our poor power to explain, it was the offering of God's only begotten Son for the sin of lost mankind. Youth see Jesus as their hero; we must help them to see him as more than that.

Jesus as Lord and Savior

Jesus is more than a hero—much, much more. Jesus must become the personal Savior and Lord of life for these same young people who have seen him as leader, teacher, and hero. It may be that in the Sunday-school class session, when the "time is ripe," the teacher can press home the claims of Jesus for a personal decision. We must teach these young people and seniors that Jesus becomes a Savior to them only when there is a personal confession of faith, a personal surrender of life, an individual acceptance of Christ.

The historic facts about Jesus are very important parts of teaching the life of Jesus, but let us not miss the most important part by failing to follow through with the ancient but ever-modern question, "What do *you* think of Jesus?" Now when seniors are making lifelong choices, and young people are casting the form which their lives will take for years to come—now is the time to lift up Jesus Christ as the one who died for their sins and their salvation, to proclaim him as the "one altogether lovely." An alert teacher will be watching for the opportune moment to help his pupils when the Spirit of God speaks softly and tenderly to their hearts. To help guide those young lives into full salvation, fellowship with God, an experience of intimate comradeship with Jesus Christ, and the joy of a forgiven and surrendered life—that is the supreme joy and privilege of the teacher.

The Teachings of Jesus

For this age group there ought to be some careful and systematic study of the teachings of Jesus. It would be helpful for seniors and young people to memorize one outline of the life of Jesus and another of his teachings. They are already acquainted with many interesting and helpful details of Jesus' life and teachings; now they need a grasp of the total in bold, broad outline.

It may be helpful to approach this systematic study indirectly. For example, the subject of war and peace is very vital to this age group. It should not be difficult to bring out such an observation as, "I wonder what Jesus taught about war, and whether his teachings could be lived out today." Young people are trying to be Christians and want to live as Jesus did in all areas of life. What would Jesus say and do about the modern problem of war and peace? That could very easily lead into a careful survey of the life and teachings of Jesus. Such a study will be most helpful if at every step it is related definitely to the problems these youth face. The same approach could be used on such other topics as labor problems, marriage, living together in a world like this, how to love one's enemies, or similar problems which young people and seniors meet day after day.

Study the Gospels

For seniors and young people a great deal of emphasis ought to be placed upon studying the Gospels themselves to get the life and teachings of Jesus. They may need guidance in discovering how all four books tell the same story in spite of their apparent differences, but it will help them to read those stories for themselves. The teacher should point out the values of a good harmony of the Gospels for comparative study.

Worship and Service

Seniors and youth are interested not only in study, but in worship and in service as well. So in teaching the life of Jesus to them one should stress both of these elements. Such questions as these will interest this age group: How did Jesus worship? What was the attitude of Jesus toward formal worship? Did Jesus teach us anything about worship? What place did prayer have in the life of Jesus? Did Jesus find in prayer anything more than "subjective value"?

The teacher of youth has a great opportunity to help them to see that the teachings of Jesus never stop at the doors of the church, but always issue in better attitudes and service. Here is a good place to use the project method in teaching. It is not enough to talk about what Jesus would do if he were here on earth today in human form; these eager young lives must be led to dedicated service in the name of Jesus.

How Jesus Made Decisions

Seniors and young people live in a turbulent world. Day after day they are faced with new situations which call for close decisions. Questions of right and wrong loom large for them. Some things are wrong in the judgment of most of the people of the world; like the traffic light the red flashes "stop" in the face of those particular things. Other matters have the approval of people generally; the green light is on. But what of those scores of decisions on which there is no clear red or green light? What of those questions to which only the yellow light of caution gives guidance? Here they should be led to see how Jesus made such decisions.

Jesus Christ becomes a real comrade to these who are going through some of the same conflicts he faced. His wilderness temptations, the decision to enter the public ministry, the intense struggle with ideals as against popularity, and the final battle and surrender to the Father in the garden—all of these crisis experiences speak to the heart and life of seniors and young people. Many of them are choosing their lifework and their life partner, and they will soon make other major decisions. The teacher can help them to make these decisions as Jesus made his major decisions. In the light of those major decisions, all the lesser choices of life will also be made.

Some of these people, perhaps, have not yet made a full commitment of their lives to Jesus Christ. It is not enough to study about Jesus; we must go on to press home his claims for full discipleship. Nothing less than a surrendered life, full salvation, and dedication to Christ should be the goal of the teacher. That will mean conversion for some. For others who have already accepted Jesus Christ as personal Savior and Lord of their lives, a study of his life and teachings will surely open new areas for a greater, deeper, and more intense dedication of all of life.

ADULTS

By the time one is an adult, if he has come up through the various departments of the church school, he should have learned much about the life and teachings of Jesus. But there is still more to learn!

Adults should have the opportunity of studying more of the historical and cultural backgrounds of the life of Jesus. They should become familiar with some of the books on the life of Jesus which have been written through the years. They should have developed some appreciation for the life of Jesus as it has appeared in music, in paintings and sculpture, in poetry and prose. Much of this will have taken place in the young people's department and should now be magnified and intensified. Adults may become interested in projects of research which will bring to the attention of the entire class historical information that illuminates the events of the life of Jesus.

Adults will also be more interested in a comparative study of the four Gospels as they treat the life and teachings of Jesus. Many of them are aware of some of the critical problems that have been discussed by New Testament scholars and will want to discover for themselves a solid foundation for their own position on such matters.

Adults should not be allowed, though, to let their study of the life of Jesus stop with a class session. The teachings of Jesus must come alive for them, too, so that personal and social life are different— *qualitatively different*—because of a Christ-centered experience. They should be led to see how the teachings of Jesus apply to the world of today, and then should be guided in projects where the theory becomes practice. They should have a comprehensive knowledge of the life of Jesus, along with detailed knowledge of much of the background of that life. They should also know the great basic principles and truths which Jesus laid down as the foundation for righteous living and discipleship.

"Thou Art the Christ"

We always learn more than we are taught. In any study of the life and teachings of Jesus, the teacher does more than impart information or guide in discovery and development. The teacher communicates something of his own faith in Jesus Christ. Something of his own fellowship with the

Christ overflows in his teaching. That quality of personal experience is probably the most important qualification in teaching the life of Jesus to other people.

There is an old story about two men who repeated the Twenty-Third Psalm before a gathering of friends. The first was a noted actor, a man of rare skill in public speaking. When he had repeated this immortal chapter from the Bible, the group of friends applauded loudly. The other man was an elderly minister. When he repeated the same passage before the same group, there followed a sacred silence. It was broken only by the actor, who said, "I know the psalm; the old pastor knows the Shepherd." Excellence in teaching the life of Jesus begins just there, in a personal knowledge and experience of Jesus Christ as the Lord and Master, Friend and Elder Brother, Savior and King.

TOPICS FOR FURTHER THOUGHT

1. If you are a teacher of children, make a list of some of the stories suitable for the age you teach.

2. Can you recall any of your early experiences as a child in which you listened to stories of the Bible? Which stories appealed to you most? From your observation of children today, to what kind of stories about Jesus do they seem to respond best?

3. What would you say to a teacher or parent who insists that all parts of the Bible can be taught to any child of any age with equal satisfaction and success?

4. If you teach juniors or intermediates you may find it helpful to give a simple test, perhaps a true-false test, to ascertain how much of the life and teaching of Jesus they know. This may give you guidance in determining what and how to teach them about Jesus.

5. What would happen in our world if we could so present Jesus Christ to young people that they would

see in him the appealing leader whom many youth movements across the world have sought in their national leaders? Are we true to our stewardship if we do not so present Jesus?

6. What place in the curriculum of an adult church-school class should there be for periodic study of the life and teachings of Jesus?